DR. DAVID SHERBINO

ESSENTIALS

EXPLORING AND UNDERSTANDING THE
ESSENTIAL BELIEFS OF THE CHRISTIAN FAITH

The Essentials: Exploring and Understanding the Essential Beliefs of the Christian Faith
Copyright ©2021 David Sherbino

Published by Castle Quay Books
Burlington, Ontario, Canada and Jupiter, Florida, U.S.A.
416-573-3249 | info@castlequaybooks.com | www.castlequaybooks.com

Edited by Marina Hofman Willard
Cover design and book interior by Burst Impressions

978-1-988928-57-9 Soft Cover
978-1-988928-58-6 E-book

Library and Archives Canada Cataloguing in Publication

    Title: The essentials : exploring and understanding the essential beliefs of the Christian faith /
  by Dr David Sherbino.
Names: Sherbino, David, author.
Identifiers: Canadiana 20210358939 | ISBN 9781988928579 (softcover)
Subjects: LCSH: Christianity.
Classification: LCC BR121.3 .S54 2021 | DDC 230—dc23

CASTLE QUAY BOOKS

USING THIS WORKBOOK

As a minister with years of experience in a congregational setting, I have discovered that many people are seeking a better understanding of the basic teachings of the Christian faith. Some have been in the church for many years, some are quite young in their faith journey, and others may be considering the Christian faith for the first time. Regardless of where you are in your faith journey, this material is designed to help you explore and understand some of the foundational teachings of the Christian faith and discover its relevance for daily life.

Some might use this material in classes that prepare individuals for membership in a local congregation, others might use it as a study guide for small groups, and there may be others who simply have a lot of questions about Christianity and want some insight and answers to their questions.

Each chapter is not intended to be a definitive statement; rather, it is a guide to explore the various topics. There is so much more that can be explored about each topic that I would encourage those who are teaching the course or leading a discussion on the various topics in a small group setting to be creative in their approach and to feel free to add to or omit material from this text.

At the end of each chapter, there are questions that relate to the topic. This is an integral part of the material that encourages participants to explore each topic further by studying applicable Scripture passages and discussing the questions. This helps the one who is leading the course see if the participants understand the material that has been taught, and it will allow for greater conversation and learning among the participants.

There are many who are interested in exploring the teachings of the Christian faith at an introductory level. Consequently, I have written at a popular level and have tried to avoid some of the more controversial theological issues. I am convinced that the material in this book is grounded in biblical orthodoxy and that most Christians would agree that these are essentials issues to be considered.

The topic of baptism includes the practice of infant baptism as well as infant dedication. This is one issue that has caused some controversary in the church. Since there are churches that practice infant baptism and others that practice infant dedication, I felt it necessary to include both. Hopefully, by examining these issues, we will better understand each position.

My desire is that this material will benefit all the people of God and ultimately enable us to grow in our relationship with Jesus, the Lord of the church.

—David Sherbino

_____

David Sherbino is Professor of Pastoral Ministries and Spiritual Formation at Tyndale University (Seminary), Toronto, Canada, and a congregational minister with the Presbyterian Church in Canada. Professionally, he is a certified spiritual director supervisor, a certified clinical thanatologist, and a fellow in thanatology. David serves as visiting professor at several seminaries in North America and overseas and speaks at numerous conferences.

He has written several books, including the award-winning books, *Re-Connect: Exercises to Develop Intimacy with God*; *Living, Dying, Living Forever: Spiritual Reflections on the Journey of Life*; and *Renew: A Basic Guide for a Personal Retreat*. All are published by Castle Quay Books.

David is an avid hockey player, an enthusiastic motorcyclist, and an out-of-control skier.

CONTENTS

1.
THE BIBLE

Introduction

One of the most important truths of the Christian faith is that God, the creator of heaven and earth, has chosen not only to communicate with us but also to live in our hearts by faith. One of the ways that he has chosen to communicate with us is through the Bible. New Testament scholar Scott McKnight writes, "The Bible has a purpose: to help you hear God speak to you. But the paper becomes the voice of the Person only when we are open to the Holy Spirit. Our God is a God who speaks, and God speaks to us through our reading of the Bible."[1]

As we begin this study we start with a brief understanding of the Bible and how to understand what God is saying to us through his word. The word *Bible* comes from the Greek word meaning "book." Therefore, the Holy Bible means the "Holy Book." The New Testament refers to the Old Testament as the Scriptures, which means "writings." Thus, one could also use the term "Holy Writings."

The Divisions of the Bible

In the Bible there are 66 books written over a period of approximately 1500 years. The books are divided into two main sections called the Old Testament and the New Testament.

The Old Testament

The Old Testament can be divided into the following categories:

---

1. Scott McKnight, *Open to the Spirit* (New York: WaterBrook, 2010), 29.

The Law

The first five books of the Old Testament contain the law of God for the nation of Israel and these five books are often referred to as the Pentateuch.

The Books of the Law (5) are:

Genesis
Exodus
Leviticus
Numbers
Deuteronomy

Historical Books

The historical books describe the initial occupation and eventual resettlement of the nation of Israel in the promised land, the transition from the rule of the judges to a monarchy, the division of the nation and the subsequent captivities of the northern and southern kingdoms, and finally the return of the remnant.

The Historical Books (12) are:

Joshua
Judges
Ruth
1 & 2 Samuel
1 & 2 Kings
1 & 2 Chronicles
Ezra
Nehemiah
Esther

Poetry and Wisdom Literature

The poetic and wisdom literature reflect the human response to all the events of life. The feelings of joy, love, despair, anguish, despondency, and hope are all captured in the pages of this literature. It is through the reality of life experiences, captured in these books that one realizes God is working out his purpose.

The books of poetic and wisdom literature (5) are:

Job
Psalms
Proverbs
Ecclesiastes
Song of Songs

Prophecy

A prophet is one who speaks God's word to the people. In the Old Testament, the prophets were to explain God's law and his promises to the people. They challenged the people to holy living and foretold of the future acts of God. In particular, the prophets foretold the coming of the Messiah, the one who was the hope of the nations. The prophetic books are divided into two categories: Major (4) and Minor (12). Some might think that a major prophet had something of greater significance to say than a minor prophet. However, that is not the case. The major prophets, though fewer in number than the minor prophets, are designated as major simply because their content is more extensive. The major prophets' work is comprised of 183 chapters, while the minor prophets is comprised of 67 chapters.

The Major Prophets (5 books) are:

Isaiah
Jeremiah
Lamentations
Ezekiel
Daniel

The Minor Prophets (12 books) are:

> Hosea
> Joel
> Amos
> Obadiah
> Jonah
> Micah
> Nahum
> Habakkuk
> Zephaniah
> Haggai
> Zechariah
> Malachi

The New Testament

The New Testament is divided into the following categories:

History

The first four books of the New Testament are called the Gospels because they refer to the good news (gospel) about Jesus. The Gospels are accounts of the life of Jesus and reveal him to be the Messiah. The fifth book, Acts of the Apostles, gives an account of the development of the early church.

The Historical books (5) are:

> Matthew
> Mark
> Luke
> John
> Acts of the Apostles

Epistles or Letters

The epistles, or letters, are a series of messages written to individuals, churches, or clusters of churches. Their primary purpose was to address issues that arose in the early church and to provide instruction and correction in living the Christian life.

The Epistles (21 books) are:

Romans
1 & 2 Corinthians
Galatians
Ephesians
Philippians
Colossians
1 & 2 Thessalonians
1 & 2 Timothy
Titus
Philemon
Hebrews
James
1 & 2 Peter
1, 2, & 3 John
Jude

Prophecy

The last book of the New Testament contains a series of visions given by God to the apostle John. The language is filled with symbolism, but throughout the ages this book has given great hope to Christians, as the message reveals that God is ultimately in control of history and that the powers of darkness will ultimately be defeated.

The book of Prophecy (1) is:

> The Revelation of John

God Speaks Through Revelation

A basic claim of the Bible is that God wants to make himself known to us. Therefore, we need to realize that Christianity is a revealed religion. God speaks to us. He speaks to us because he desires to be in a relationship with us. There are different ways that God reveals himself, some of which are described here.

General Revelation

General revelation, sometimes referred to as natural revelation, is one of the ways God makes himself known to all people through creation, through the natural law, or through reasoning. Three things we discover about God through general revelation are the following:

We discover God's eternity, power, and divinity.

> The *heavens* declare the glory of God; the skies proclaim the work of his hands. (Psalm 19:1, emphasis added)

> For *since* the creation of the world God's invisible qualities—his eternal power and divine nature—have been clearly seen, being understood from what has been made, so that people are without excuse. (Romans 1:20, emphasis added)

We discover God's kindness.

> He has *shown* you kindness by giving you rain from heaven and crops in their seasons; he provides you with plenty of food and fills your hearts with joy. (Acts 14:17, emphasis added)

We discover God's moral law.

> All who *sin* apart from the law will also perish apart from the law, and all who sin under the law will be judged by the law. (Romans 2:12, emphasis added)

Special Revelation

God has chosen to speak to all people through creation to make himself known as Creator. However, it is through special revelation that he makes himself known as Saviour. This act of special revelation comes through prophets, through the Scriptures, and ultimately through Jesus Christ.

A major factor of special revelation is that God spoke. "In the past God spoke to our ancestors through the prophets at many times and in various ways, but in these last days he has spoken to us by his Son, whom he appointed heir of all things and through whom he made the universe" (Hebrews 1:1–2).

In the Old Testament, the prophets who spoke often prefaced their statement with the words "This is what the LORD says," which implied that the words spoken by them were not simply their words but were to be received as God's words (2 Peter 1:21).

The ultimate expression of God's revelation is in his Son, Jesus.

> That which was from the beginning, which we have heard, which we have seen with our eyes, which we have looked at and our hands have touched—this we proclaim concerning the Word of life. The life appeared and we have seen it and testify to it, and we proclaim to you the eternal life, which was with the Father and has appeared to us. We proclaim to you what we have seen and heard so that you also may have fellowship with us. And our fellowship is with the Father and with his Son, Jesus Christ. We write this to make our joy complete. This is the message we have heard from him and declare to you: God is light; in him there is no darkness at all. (1 John 1:1–5)

The Inspiration of the Bible

Although written over a period of about 1500 years, the Bible maintains that God is the ultimate author speaking through various writers. Thus, it is customary to use the term *inspiration* when one refers to the origin of the Bible.

> All Scripture is God breathed [inspired] and is useful for teaching, rebuking, correcting and training in righteousness, so that the servant of God may be thoroughly equipped for every good work. (2 Timothy 3:16–17)

Inspiration is not the same as the idea conveyed when one declares "that was an inspiring lecture or that was an inspiring song." Theologian J. I. Packer states, "Inspiration means 'God breathed' and is defined as a supernatural, providential influence of God's Holy Spirit upon the human authors which caused them to write what He wished to be written for the communication of revealed truth to others."[2]

The Jewish people and the New Testament writers accepted that the Old Testament Scriptures were inspired by God. Jesus upheld that view, and when he quoted from the Old Testament Scriptures, he regarded them as being the words of God: "Above all you must understand that no prophecy of Scripture came about by the prophet's own interpretation of things. For prophecy never had its origin in the human will, but prophets, though human, spoke as they were carried along by the Holy Spirit" (2 Peter 1:20–21).

At the same time, it is recognized that the writers of the Scriptures, both the Old and New Testament, came from a variety of backgrounds. They came from different cultures, from different time periods, and with different intellectual abilities. They were not robots that simply recorded words given to them by God; rather, God spoke through the uniqueness of their personalities and circumstances to communicate his message to people.

When we read the Bible, it is important to realize that it is the word of God speaking to us. The psalmist wrote these words thousands of years ago, but it is still God speaking to us today.

> The law of the LORD is perfect, refreshing the soul. The statutes of the Lord are trustworthy, making wise the simple. The precepts of the LORD are right, giving joy to the heart. The commands of

---

2. J. I. Packer, *Fundamentalism and the Word of God* (London: InterVarsity Press, 1977), 77.

the Lord are radiant, giving light to the eyes. The fear of the Lord is pure, enduring forever. The decrees of the Lord are firm, and all of them are righteous. They are more precious than gold, than much pure gold; they are sweeter than honey, than honey from the honeycomb. By them is your servant warned; in keeping them there is great reward. (Psalm 19:7–11)

We need to realize the Bible is a book that we can trust and that it will impact our life in many ways. Try the following exercise, and discover how God's word talks about God's word.

Exercise: Read the following passages, and write down what each one says about how your life could be affected by God's word.

Joshua 1:8

Psalm 119:28

John 17:17

2 Timothy 2:15

1 Timothy 4:13, 15

Basic Principles of Interpretation

The science of biblical interpretation is called hermeneutics. This implies there are certain guidelines that need to be followed when interpreting the Bible.

The Analogy of Faith

The most basic principle of interpretation is the analogy of faith. Theologian R. C. Sproul contends that this means Scripture is to be interpreted by Scripture. In other words, passages of Scripture are to be interpreted in the light of the whole of the Bible. Passages of Scripture that are difficult to understand or seem to present a conflicting point of view are to be interpreted in the light of that which is known.[3]

Literal Interpretation

Some have misunderstood the meaning of literal interpretation. For example, when Jesus said he was the Good Shepherd, it is clear that this was not to be taken literally in the sense that he was referring to his occupation. Jesus was not a shepherd; he was a carpenter. To interpret the Bible literally means that the passage is to be understood in the normal sense according to the rules of grammar and context. Much of the time, grammatical structure tells us whether the words are in the form of a command, question, or declaration. The historical context helps us have a better understanding of the original meaning to the first readers. Consequently, the more modern readers know about the times and customs of the biblical era, the clearer the meaning of the text becomes for them.

---

3. R. C. Sproul, *Knowing Scripture* (Downers Grove: InterVarsity Press, 1977), 47.

The Holy Spirit as Interpreter

Since the Scriptures reveal spiritual truths, to understand these truths there must be a spiritual awareness and receptivity. The apostle Paul writes, "The person without the Spirit does not accept the things that come from the Spirit of God but considers them foolishness, and cannot understand them, because they are discerned only through the Spirit" (1 Corinthians 2:14). Thus, without spiritual enlightenment by the Holy Spirit, we will not comprehend spiritual truth. It is the work of the Holy Spirit to open our minds to biblical truth (John 14:26; 16:13–14).

Theologian and author J. I. Packer states that in our study of Scripture we "must approach … in humble dependence on the Holy Spirit, sure that we can learn nothing of spiritual significance unless we are taught of God. Confidence in one's own powers of discernment is an effective barrier to spiritual understanding."[4]

Practical Applications

Step One: Preparation

Approach the study of Scripture prayerfully. The Scriptures deal with issues that involve every aspect of our life. To approach the study prayerfully implies we are willing to act obediently to God's Word (Psalm 119:33–40).

Step Two: Observation

Observe what is taking place in the passage. Don't read too quickly. Take time to note the various details. What is the general tone of the passage? How does the writer address the readers? Look at the literary form of the passage. Is it discourse, narrative, poetic, dramatic, parabolic, or apocalyptic? Be alert for admonitions that the writer gives. Are there promises or words of encouragement? Watch for imperative words.

Finally, watch for the use of questions. Is the question used to introduce an idea, summarize a series of ideas, or just to challenge your thinking?

---

4. Packer, *Fundamentalism and the Word of God*, 112.

Step Three: Interpretation

An interpretation asks the question "What does it mean?" Recognize the style of writing the author is using. It may be poetry, wisdom literature, allegory, parable, or historical narrative. Each style brings new insight to the context. Consider the historical context of the passage. Be careful not to draw conclusions the author did not intend to convey.

Ask interpretive questions.
What is the importance of
> a key word?
> a key phrase?
> names and titles?
> Why did the author say this?
> What is the context before and after the passage you are studying?

Step Four: Application

Application asks the question "How does this affect or relate to my life?" This part of the Bible study process takes the truths that have been discovered/observed and incorporates them into our daily lives. Jesus said it is not enough just to hear his words; we must do what they say (James 1:22–25), as this is wisdom (Matthew 7:24–27).

Step Five: Read All the Bible

There is a tendency to read only favourite passages or to rely on verses we have learned in the past. Spiritual maturity depends upon knowing the whole counsel of God. We need to have a broad understanding of all that the Bible teaches on a given subject (Colossians 3:16).

Bible Study Tools

There are many helpful and practical study tools to assist you in your study of the Bible.

- A Bible commentary—single volume or set
- Bible dictionary
- Bible handbook

DISCUSSION QUESTIONS TO EXPLORE THE IMPORTANCE OF THE BIBLE

The following questions are designed to help you understand the significance of the Bible in your daily life. Take time to read the different passages and reflect on the questions. Be prepared to explore these questions further when your group meets.

Read Psalm 119:97–114.

This passage will give you some insights into the importance of the Bible for daily living.

1-1 List some of the benefits that will result from meditating on the Scriptures. Expand on one that is of particular interest to you.

1-2 In verse 105 God's word is described as a lamp for your feet and a light on your path. What does that mean? How have you experienced this reality in your life?

1-3 In verse 114 the writer states he has put his hope in God's word. What hope would one receive from God's word? Has this been your experience in any situation?

Read 2 Timothy 3:16–17.

1-4 What does this passage tell you about the reliability and significance of the Bible?

1-5 Note the origin and purpose.

Read Mark 4:1–20.

1-6 Describe the four types of soil on which the seeds fell. What was the growth on the different types of ground?

1-7 Jesus was speaking in a parable. A parable was a method used by Jesus whereby he told a story to illustrate a spiritual lesson. The soil in this parable represents different types of lifestyles. How do the different people respond to the word of God? What seems to be the reason for the different responses?

1-8 Take a moment to think about your life. What type of soil would best describe you when you heard the gospel for the first time? What type of soil do you think your life represents now? Can you describe what that is like?

1-9 In the light of this study, what is one thing you would like to ask of God as you continue your journey of life?

2.
THE NATURE OF GOD

Introduction

In this age of pluralism when there is an acceptance of many religions, various deities that people worship, and just as many opinions about the nature of God, the Bible claims to be the revelation of the one true God. There is no attempt in the Bible to prove the existence of God; it simply states his existence. God has no beginning or ending—he simply is. The reality of this, states theologian Louis Berkhof, is "as the self-existent God, He is not only independent in Himself, but also causes everything to depend upon Him."[5]

The Character and Attributes of God

The Name of God

God has revealed himself and made known to us his name. When God told Moses to go and speak to Pharaoh and tell him that the God of his fathers had sent him to free the Israelites, Moses then asked, "What do I say when they ask me his name?" God replied, "I AM WHO I AM" (Exodus 3:14). The name of God, YHWH (Yahweh), means I AM WHO I AM. This name, according to theologian J. I. Packer, "declares God's almightiness: he cannot be hindered from being what he is and doing what he wills."[6]

There are other names of God that reveal different aspects of his person. The following names are simply a few that belong to God:

---

5. Louis Berkhof, *Systematic Theology* (Grand Rapids: Eerdmans, 1965), 58.
6. J. I. Packer, *I Want to Be a Christian* (Wheaton: Tyndale, 1977), 28.

Jehovah-Shammah—The LORD is there (Ezekiel 48:35)

Jehovah-Rohi—The LORD is my shepherd (Psalm 23:1)

Jehovah-Jireh—The LORD will provide (Genesis 22:14)

Jehovah-Rophe (more commonly Rapha)—The LORD is my healer (Exodus 15:26)

Jehovah-Tsidkenu—The LORD is our righteous saviour / God is my righteousness (Jeremiah 23:6)

Jehovah-M'Kaddish—The LORD who makes you holy (Leviticus 20:8)

Jehovah-Shalom—The LORD is peace (Judges 6:24)

Jehovah-Nissi—The LORD is my banner (Exodus 17:15)

These different names for God are revealed in various situations and circumstances. As you study these passages, you will have a greater appreciation of the nature of God, how he interacts with his people, and this will enable you to praise him more fully.

The Attributes of God

When we speak about the attributes of God, we refer to those perfections or characteristics of God revealed in the Bible. At times these are difficult to comprehend.

Communicable and Incommunicable Attributes

The attributes of God are divided into two categories. Communicable attributes refer to those characteristics of God that are shared by humankind (e.g., goodness, kindness, and mercy). Incommunicable attributes refer to those characteristics that are unique to God alone and are not shared by people (e.g., self-existence, the infinity of God).

Exercise 2–1

From the following list which attributes would you consider to be communicable and uncommunicable?

Infinite	Just
Holy	Omniscient
Unchanging	Good

Omnipresent	Self existent
Loving	Wise
Sovereign	True
Merciful	Omnipotent

The Uniqueness of God's Being

Consider some of the following incommunicable attributes of God.

Omnipresent: God Is Everywhere

The omnipresence of God refers to the fact that God is everywhere. However, we must caution against the error of pantheism, which suggest that the being of God is the substance of all things. In pantheism we see the worship of nature, but nature is not God, and God is not in all of nature. For example, in Psalm 24:1 we read, "The earth is the Lord's." Pantheism would state, "The earth is the Lord."

However, the Bible does teach that there is nowhere in the world that one can be absent from the presence of God (Psalm 139:7–12).

One must be careful not to limit God in the way he is present among people. Authors Bewes and Hicks state, "He is present creatively in his works; he is present morally in the area of human behaviour; he is present spiritually among his people; he is present sovereignly in nations, governments and systems."[7]

Omniscient: God Knows Everything

This truth refers to the fact that the knowledge of God is perfect and all comprehensive.

> He is perfect in knowledge. (Job 37:16)
> He is able to observe the ways of people. (Deuteronomy 2:7)
> He knows the days of our life. (Psalm 139:16)

---

7. Richard Bewes and Robert Hicks, *Explaining Bible Truth* (Middlesex: Creative Publishing, 1981), 7.

Most people gain knowledge from others, but God's knowledge is eternal.

Omnipotent: God Is All-Powerful

The concept of omnipotence does not imply that God can do anything. In fact, there are certain things that God cannot do simply because of his nature. Consequently, he cannot act out of his character, which implies he cannot forgive sin without atonement, he can't lie, and he can't be inconsistent.

We can see some examples of the power of God revealed in his acts of creation, in his judgment of people (Psalm 75:7; Job 42:1–2), and in the fact that ultimately, he will subdue evil (Jeremiah 32:17) and restore the world (Revelation 21:5; Isaiah 35).

Some suggest that the presence of evil indicates that God is not all-powerful, because if he were all-powerful, then evil would be eradicated. Note how the following passages enable you to address this concern (Romans 8:18–23; 2 Peter 3:3–10).

The Character of God

Goodness, holiness, and righteousness delineate three major characteristics of God.

The Goodness of God

There are several aspects of this characteristic as revealed in his kindness, love and grace.

The Kindness of God

God's kindness is seen in relation to all creation. The psalmist declared, "The Lord is good to all; he has compassion on all he has made" (Psalm 145:9). Further expressions of God's kindness are seen in various texts, including Psalm 145:15–16 and Luke 6:35, where we see his interest in meeting our needs.

The Love of God

There is a love of God for all creation. God recognizes even the sinner who might reject the Creator as a person who has been created in his image and likeness, although this image has been marred (John 3:16; Matthew 5:44–45).

However, there is a special love of God toward those he has called to be his children. To these God has given his saving love to the full extent (John 16:27; 1 John 3:1).

The Grace of God

Grace implies favour one shows toward another. Biblically speaking, when we speak of the grace of God, we stress that it is the gift of God's kindness toward humankind that is not deserved.

Theologians speak of two aspects of grace: common grace and saving grace.

Common grace is the unmerited favour of God toward all people. An example of common grace is demonstrated in acts where God restrains sin so that law and order are maintained. Thus, government is an element of common grace (Romans 13:6). Common grace is seen when God sends the rain to fall on both the just and the unjust (Matthew 5:45).

Saving grace is the special grace of God whereby, according to theologian Berkhof, God removes "the guilt and penalty of sin, changes the inner life of the individual, and gradually cleanses the person from the pollution of sin."[8] (See Ephesians 1:6–7; 2:7–9; Titus 2:11.) J. I. Packer defines saving grace as "God's underserved favour. Therefore, God's love for humankind is a gift from God, undeserved by people and dependent only upon God's will."[9]

We need to understand that if the saving grace of God reveals humanity as guilty in its sin and in need of forgiveness, then the mercy of God shows the compassion of God as he offers forgiveness. The Bible states that God is slow to punish sin, as he desires all people to repent and turn from their wrongdoing (Psalm 57:10; 2 Peter 3:9).

---

8. Berkhof, *Systematic Theology*, 439.
9. J. I. Packer, *God's Word* (Downers Grove: InterVarsity Press, 1981), 97.

The Holiness of God

The holiness of God essentially refers to the aspect of the nature of God that separates him from all others. The word *holy* means "set apart" or "separate from." The Bible states, "There is no one holy like the LORD" (1 Samuel 2:2). Since God is holy, he is completely committed to goodness and cannot have anything to do with evil. We need to enter his presence with reverence (Isaiah 6:1–5; Habakkuk 1:13; Revelation 15:4).

The Righteousness of God

The aspect of righteousness in God's nature is closely related to the holiness of God. The term implies an adherence to a law or standard. When we think of righteousness, we often refer to a life that is pleasing to God. In relation to God, theologian Berkhof declares that God is infinitely righteous in himself.[10] But God also reveals a righteousness in dealing with humankind, and in this regard, it is spoken of in terms of his justice being righteous (Psalm 119:137; John 17:25; 1 John 2:29; 3:7).

The Trinity

One of the great mysteries of the Christian faith is that although there is only one God, he is revealed in three distinct persons. This is referred to as the tri-unity of God. From the outset, I want to state very clearly this is a difficult doctrine to understand. However, the teaching that God is three persons in one substance is simply an attempt to explain what is revealed in the Bible.

The common designations of the three persons in the Trinity are Father, Son, and Holy Spirit. It is acknowledged there is no such word as trinity in the Bible, but when the Bible is examined, several factors about the relationship between the three members of the godhead emerge.

In the Old Testament, in Genesis 1:26, God says, "Let us make mankind in our image, in our likeness," which may be indicating the three-in-one nature of the Trinity. In exploring the Old Testament, one discovers numerous references to various members of the Trinity, which would indicate three persons in the godhead (Genesis 3:22–24; 11:6–7; 1 Samuel 16:13; Daniel 7:13–14).

---

10. Berkhof, *Systematic Theology*, 436.

In the New Testament, we see a greater distinction between the Father, the Son, and the Holy Spirit. For example, divine attributes are given to the Son and to the Holy Spirit. Paul referenced Jesus, the Son of God, as "the image of the invisible God, the firstborn over-all creation. For in him all things were created: things in heaven and on earth, visible and invisible … all things have been created through him and for him. He is before all things and in him all things hold together" (Colossians 1:15–17). Kathryn Turner, a theologian, states, "Jesus relates to the Father, the first Person of the Trinity, in the mode of existence of the Son, the second Person of the Trinity, made human."[11]

Concerning the Holy Spirit, John conveys the promise Jesus offered.

> "If you love me, keep my commands. And I will ask the Father, and he will give you another advocate to help you and to be with you forever—the Spirit of truth. The world cannot accept him, because it neither sees him nor knows him. But you know him, for he lives with you and will be in you." (John 14:15–17)

There are different ways in which the three persons of the Godhead relate to each other. Authors Richard Bewes and Robert Hicks suggest that the term *Father*, the first person of the Trinity, is not about his relationship to creation but to his relationship with the eternal Son. The Son, the second person of the Trinity, became human in the person of Jesus Christ, in order to rescue humankind from sin. As the Son, he shares in the Father's glory but is subordinate to the Father only because of the work he does. The Son only acted under the authority of the Father. The Holy Spirit, the third person of the Trinity, was sent from the Father to make personal what Christ made available to us through the cross. Just as Christ once lived among us now the Holy Spirit lives in the life of every believer (Matthew 10:40; Galatians 4:4; John 15:26; 16:14).[12]

The Westminster Shorter Catechism—a confession of faith in the Reformed tradition—understands that the relationship between the members of the Trinity does not imply inequality. Rather the members of the godhead are the same in substance, equal in power and glory.

---

11. Kathryn Turner, *Jesus Humanity and the Trinity* (Minneapolis: Fortress Press, 2001), 32.
12. Bewes and Hicks, *Explaining Bible Truth*, 19.

In their relationship all members of the godhead work together in

> Creation (Genesis 1:1)
> Incarnation (Luke 1:35)
> Baptism (Matthew 28:18–20)
> Atonement (Hebrews 9:14)
> Resurrection (Acts 2:32; John 10:17–18; Romans 1:4)

Ultimately, this teaching about the Trinity is accepted by seeing the work of God the Father, God the Son, and God the Holy Spirit in the Bible and in our lives. We do not rely on proof texts, but as we study the Bible, we will see the truth of the Trinity running throughout the whole of Scripture.

DISCUSSION QUESTIONS TO EXPLORE THE NATURE OF GOD

This study is designed to help you explore in more detail various aspects of the nature of God.

Read Psalm 139.

2–1. Verses 1–6: What is the main idea you discover about God? How does this knowledge impact your relationship with God?

2–2. Verses 7–12: Have you ever felt that you would like to run away from God? Why? Why not? Does the fact that God is present in every circumstance give you any encouragement, comfort, or hope?

2–3. Verses 13–18: How does this passage speak about your significance in the eyes of God? How will this impact the way you live each day, especially the way you treat others?

2–4. Verses 23–24: Why do you think the author asks God to search his thoughts? What would be the outcome of such a request? Does this speak to your relationship with God? If so, how does it impact your life?

Read Psalm 103.

This psalm is filled with various reasons to give praise to God.

2–5. Take some time to read this passage, and then list some of the significant characteristics of God that are mentioned in this psalm.

2–6. Having listed some of the characteristics of God's nature, take a few minutes to reflect on several of them, and write out in your own words a short prayer of praise to God.

Read John 14:5–21.

2–7. What does this passage tell you about the relationship between Jesus and the Father? Does it give you any insight into the working of the Holy Trinity? Consider verses 9–11 and 15–21.

2–8. Verses 12–14: Do you think the promises given by Jesus are like a blank cheque, or are there conditions attached to them? If there are conditions, what are they?

3.
JESUS CHRIST

Introduction

Jesus is the center of the Christian faith. The claims that he makes about himself and the evidence to verify those claims indicate that he is truly God and man. It is these unique claims that set him apart from all others.

The Names of Christ

In Scripture, there are five names that are given to Christ. These names describe his office and the work he came to do.

Jesus

Jesus, the name most are familiar with, is the Greek name for Joshua, which means "God is Saviour." This is the proper name that identifies him as an historical individual who was born in Bethlehem and grew up in the village of Nazareth, where he worked as a carpenter, before beginning his three years of ministry. After a conversation with Joseph by the angel Gabriel, Matthew recorded this part of the conversation. "She [Mary] will give birth to a son, and you are to give him the name Jesus, because he will save his people from their sins" (Matthew 1:21).

Christ

Many assume that Christ is the surname of Jesus, when in fact it is a description of his ministry. The terms *Messiah* (from Hebrew) and *Christ* (from Greek) both mean "Anointed One." Jesus Christ could be described as Jesus's official name in that it is a description of his office. He is the one anointed by God to be the "Christ" (John 1:41), the "Saviour of the World" (Luke 2:11).

Son of Man

This was Jesus's most common self-designation and is found in all four Gospels. Initially one might think this term refers strictly to the humanity of Jesus. Jesus used this term in his interaction with people, since the term *Son of Man* can simply mean "human being." The Scriptures teach that Jesus was conceived by the Holy Spirit but born of a woman. His humanity enables him to identify with all of us. However, the term *Son of Man* is also a reference to his deity. The Old Testament speaks of the Son of Man who rules an everlasting kingdom (Daniel 7:9–14). The designation *Son of Man* was associated with Messiah. Consequently, this term, as used by Jesus, refers to his earthly ministry, his death, and his coming again in power and glory (Matthew 8:19–20; 17:17–21; 24:30).

Son of God

This name is used to denote the deity of Jesus. Even though he taught people to refer to God as Father, he saw his own relationship with the Father as quite different and distinct. In the Gospel of John, there are several instances where this occurred. On one occasion, Jesus healed a lame man on the Sabbath. We read what Jesus said to the religious authorities: "'My Father is always at his work to this very day, and I too am working.' For this reason, the Jews tried all the harder to kill him; not only was he breaking the Sabbath, but he was even calling God his own Father, making himself equal with God" (John 5:17–18). This understanding of Jesus's divinity is further elaborated in various texts (see John 20:17 and 32). The first hearers would have understood these texts as indicating that Jesus was claiming to be one with God the Father.

Lord

In the Old Testament, the term Lord (translated from the Hebrew *Adonai*) refers to a ruler. When this title is in capitals, as in Lord, it represents the sacred name of God. The term *God* (translated from the Hebrew *Elohim*) simply means the "Mighty One." The term *Lord* used in the New Testament also means Jehovah. When the term *Lord* is applied to Jesus it carries three connotations, depending on the context.

> 1. It is used as a polite or reverent form of addressing Jesus. A man with leprosy came, knelt before Jesus, and said, "Lord, if you are willing, you can make me clean" (Matthew 8:2).

2. It is used as an expression of authority. When Jesus was preparing to enter Jerusalem prior to his crucifixion, he sent two disciples to get a donkey and her colt to ride on as he entered the city. Matthew, in his Gospel, writes, "If anyone says anything to you, say that the Lord needs them, and he will send them right away" (Matthew 21:3).

3. Lord is used as a sign of authority expressing equivalence to God. At the annunciation of the birth of Jesus to the shepherds, we read, "Today in the town of David a Saviour has been born to you; he is the Messiah, the Lord" (Luke 2:11). We see the term *Lord* being used as part of the basic confession of the early church when they made the declaration "Jesus is Lord." This is also referenced in the hymn by the apostle Paul in his writing to the church in Philippi when he declares, "At the name of Jesus every knee should bow, in heaven and on earth and under the earth, and every tongue acknowledge that Jesus Christ is Lord, to the glory of God the Father" (Philippians 2:10–11).

The Two Natures of Jesus

The church has confessed the two natures of Christ: that he is both God and human. Philosophically, it cannot be explained how one can be both human and divine. However, the evidence for this truth is presented in Scripture in such a convincing manner that, as a believer, one learns to hold this truth in a tension.

The Humanity of Christ

It cannot be denied that Jesus was an historical figure. We know Jesus was not an abstract concept or myth, but a man who lived in a specific context, at a specific period in history, who died after a life spent on earth ministering to people for a period of about three years. Other religions, such as ancient Greek mythology, tell stories about gods who walked on the earth giving the impression they were human yet at any time they could change themselves into animals or other things.[13] It is easy to recognize the mythological aspect of such claims.

There are non-Christian writers who provide evidence about the life of Jesus, in addition to the New Testament writers. One such example is Josephus, a Jewish historian who lived from 37 to 100 CE; he made two references of Jesus.

---

13. Lee Strobel, *The Case for Christ* (Grand Rapids: Zondervan, 1998), 101.

In the New Testament, we read that God took on the fullness of our humanity and became man. This is called the incarnation. Paul expresses it this way: "When the set time had fully come, God sent his Son, born of a woman, born under the law" (Galatians 4:4). John the apostle writes, "The Word became flesh and made his dwelling among us. We have seen his glory, the glory of the one and only Son, who came from the Father, full of grace and truth" (John 1:14).

His Early Life

There are very few recorded accounts of the early life of Jesus. There is the story of his birth, which was quite normal. As mentioned above, he was conceived by the Holy Spirit—a unique event. The only other biblical account of his early years was an incident in the temple when he was twelve years old (Luke 2:41–52). This passage includes the statement that Jesus grew in wisdom, stature, and favour with God and people.

His Lifestyle and Development

As we look at the life of Jesus, it becomes evident that his development as an individual was quite normal.

1. He was obedient to his parents (Luke 2:51).
2. He had the basic needs of hunger, thirst, and rest (Matthew 4:2; 11:19; John 4:6).
3. He experienced deep emotions, such as anger, sadness, joy, disappointment, and compassion (John 11:34–35; Matthew 9:36; Mark 3:5).
4. He developed in a very normal fashion (Luke 2:40–52; Hebrews 2:18; 5:8).
5. He was limited by the factors of time and space. In other words, he could only be in one place at a time (John 11:1–6).

He Was Subject to Temptation but Was Sinless

The Bible testifies to the sinlessness of Jesus. Never once does Jesus make a confession of sin, nor is anyone able to convict him of sin. There is ample evidence that Jesus was tempted. At the very beginning of his ministry, he was forty days alone in the wilderness, where he was tempted by the devil. We see at the conclusion of his ministry, Jesus was tempted in the garden of Gethsemane to abandon his mission (Matthew 4:1–11; Luke 22:39–45).

In all the temptations he faced, Jesus was without sin. This is a unique feature about him. His conception by the Holy Spirit insures his deity and sinless nature. Being born of a woman ensures his humanity. Consequently, this enables him to be our Saviour, for only a sinless one could die for the sins of humanity. He is the perfect sacrifice (Romans 5:8–11, 18–19).

He Experienced Suffering

In his humanity, Jesus identifies with us in our suffering. In some instances, his suffering was emotional. We see that he was deserted by his friends and even one of his closest disciples, Peter, denied ever knowing him. In other instances, it was physical suffering. It is hard to imagine the pain and agony Jesus experienced when he was crucified (Matthew 27:27–50).

Through his sufferings, we are given strength and courage and hope to face the challenges of life we face (1 Peter 2:21; Hebrews 2:16–18).

The Deity of Jesus

There are many who perceive Jesus to be not only a good and kind person but also an ethical teacher. But that is it. They are not prepared to acknowledge him as God. However, as we explore the Bible, we find ample evidence to conclude that Jesus is God.

The Claims of Jesus

In the Bible, Jesus makes many egocentric claims, including that he and the Father were one (John 10:30).

He also claimed that he alone had the power to forgive sins. If this was not true, then he would be guilty of blasphemy. In fact, there are several occasions where he forgave people of their sins (Mark 2:5, 7). In several of these incidents, Jesus performed a miracle to prove that he had the authority to forgive sins (John 10:22–39).

He claimed that on the Last Day, he alone has the prerogative to be the judge of humankind (John 5:25–29).

He claimed to be able to meet the deepest needs of the human heart (Matthew 11:28–30).

He claimed to be the sustenance of life and said that without him people would never experience the abundant life he offered (John 6:35; 10:10).

He called people to make a commitment to him. Throughout history, leaders have called people to make a commitment, but it is a commitment to a cause. Jesus makes the most demanding commitment: a commitment of our life totally and unreservedly to him. This commitment takes priority over any other commitment we have in life (Luke 14:26; Mark 8:34).

The Miracles of Jesus

In the Gospels, we discover many of the miracles that Jesus performed during his ministry on earth. Not every event was recorded, but those selected were to show his power over the elements and his love and compassion toward people, to reveal his identity as the Son of God, and to make known the coming of the kingdom of God. Here are some examples:

> Healing the sick (Matthew 8:14–15)
> Casting out evil spirits (Mark 1:32)
> Turning water into wine (John 2:1–11)
> Raising the dead (Luke 7:11–17)

At the conclusion of his writing, John declares his purpose for recording the various miraculous events accomplished by Jesus: to enable the reader to believe that "Jesus is the Messiah, the Son of God, and that by believing you may have life in his name" (John 20:31).

His Manner of Life

When one considers the claims of Jesus and examines his life, there is an amazing consistency. Jesus claimed to have an intimacy with God that was not shared with anyone else. He also claimed to have an authority over people. His conduct was balanced, and it is evident that he had a spirit of humility. He associated with people from various socio-economic backgrounds; he mingled with the rich and poor alike. In everything he did, it becomes obvious that he truly cared about people and sought to serve them.

The Significance of Jesus as the God-Man

As we explore Scripture, there are several basic features that reveal the purpose of the two natures of Jesus.

He Is Our Mediator

Jesus is the one who "stands" between God and us. Because of his sinless humanity, he intervened on our behalf to present us without fault before God the Father (1 Timothy 2:5).

He Is Our Example

As we live our lives, Jesus is the example we are to follow. As we consider his life, as depicted in the Gospels, we see how one can live life to the full and in a manner that is not only pleasing to God but is considerate of others (1 Peter 2:21–23).

He Is Our Sacrifice

Scripture states, "The wages of sin is death, but the gift of God is eternal life in Christ Jesus our Lord" (Romans 6:23). Jesus is the only one who can pay the penalty for our sins since he is the only one who is sinless. Theologian C. C. Ryrie wrote, "God does not die. So, the Saviour must be human in order to be able to die. But the death of an ordinary man would not pay for sin eternally, so the Saviour must also be God."[14] (See Hebrews 10:9–10.)

He Is the One Who Gives Life

There are people who wonder if the life we have here on earth is all there is. There is in our hearts a desire for more. The writer of Ecclesiastes declares that God has "set eternity in the human heart" (3:11). It is through Jesus's death and resurrection from the dead that we can have the assurance of life that is eternal. He has conquered death and offers eternal life to all who turn to him. This is God's gift to us—eternal life (John 10:28–30).

---

14. Charles Ryrie, *So Great Salvation* (Wheaton: Victor Books, 1990), 245.

He Is Our High Priest

Jesus is the one who knows and understands everything we experience and need in life. In the book of Hebrews Jesus is referred to as our High Priest (Hebrews 2:17). One function of the High Priest was to approach God once a year to offer sacrifice for the sins of the people. Another function of the High Priest was to offer the prayers of the people to God. Jesus is our high priest. Through his sacrificial death Jesus was offered as the one, perfect, never-to-be-repeated sacrifice for the sins of all people in all times and places. Now he continually prays on our behalf before the presence of God. That is why we offer our prayers through Jesus, for he is our High Priest presenting our prayers before God the Father (Hebrews 4:14–16).

Two Heresies

The divinity and humanity of Jesus have not been acknowledged by all. The heresy of denying the divinity of Jesus is called Arianism. Arius was a teacher in the fourth century who taught that Jesus was not divine but that rather he was created by God and was the first act of creation. Thus, Jesus is viewed as a created being with some divine attributes. In Scripture, there are references to Jesus as the firstborn (Romans 8:28–30; Colossians 1:15–20). However, we must remember that this term is a reference to a place of honour in the family. It is not a reference to being created. Arianism is still with us today and is a view held by groups such as Jehovah's Witnesses.

The other heresy is called Docetism, which denies the humanity of Jesus. From this perspective, the Docetists taught that though Jesus seemed to be human, because he was divine, he could not be human. The problem with this view, in the minds of the early church fathers, was that if Jesus was not fully human, then he could not die for our sins as the perfect sacrifice. The Docetists believed matter was inherently evil, and the spirit alone was good. James Boice, a pastor and theologian, reflects on this perspective and states that if one believes this, then "the incarnation would be impossible. How could a holy God take upon himself a sinful body?"[15] As one explores Scripture, it is easy to refute this heresy.

In our study of the two natures of Jesus we must learn to hold the truth of his humanity and deity in tension.

---

15. J. Boice, *God the Redeemer* (Madison: InterVarsity Press, 1978), 141.

Conclusion

As we seek to know who Jesus we must come to some conclusion about him and who he claims to be. C. S. Lewis, author and apologist, suggested there are only three alternatives: Jesus is either a liar or a madman, or else he is telling the truth. What do you believe?

DISCUSSION QUESTIONS ABOUT THE PERSON OF JESUS CHRIST

This study will enable you to explore more fully the person of Jesus and your relationship with him.

Read Matthew 16:13–20.

3–1. Caesarea Philippi was a place known for its plurality of deities. Why would people think Jesus was John the Baptist or Elijah or Jeremiah? What do these comments reveal about the general perception people had about him?

3–2. What is significant about Peter's declaration in verse 16? What does it mean?

3–3. How did you come to recognize that Jesus was the Messiah? How has he impacted your life?

3–4. The New Testament reveals that Jesus is God. List some aspects of Jesus's divinity revealed in the following passages.

John 1:1–13

John 8:50–58

John 20:26–29

Luke 5:20–21

3–5. The New Testament claims that Jesus was not only divine but also human. What do the following texts reveal about the humanity of Jesus?

Matthew 4:1–11

Matthew 8:23–27

Hebrews 2:14–18; 5:7–8

3–6. Why do you think it is important to hold to the truth that Jesus is both God and human?

3–7. How does this dual nature of Jesus set him apart from all other religious leaders? Consider John 14:6. What are the implications of this claim for you? Does it help you grasp the significance of who Jesus is?

4.
THE HOLY SPIRIT

Introduction

The Holy Spirit is referred to as the third person of the Holy Trinity. The words of the Nicene Creed declare, "The Holy Spirit, the Lord and Giver of Life, proceeds from the Father and the Son, who with the Father and the Son together is worshipped and glorified."[16] The primary work of the Holy Spirit is to carry out the will of the Father, to reveal the Son and to work in the lives of God's people.

As we explore the role and relationship of the Holy Spirit in our life, it seems that most Christians are more familiar with the role and relationship they have with God the Father and God the Son.

Theologian and author Ken Boa states, "The role of the Holy Spirit as a central dynamic of Christian spirituality is an expression of the trinitarian life of God. The Father sent the Son into the world and empowered him by anointing him with the Spirit."[17] Boa also states that in the life of the believer, the Holy Spirit "empowers us to live a new quality of life, he purifies and purges us as we submit to his authority and control and he equips us with spiritual gifts and opportunities to build up others in the faith."[18] Elaborating on this theme, theologian Michael Reeves states,

> The life the Spirit gives is not an abstract package of blessing; it is his own life that he shares with us, the life of fellowship with the Father and the Son. Thus the Spirit is not like some divine milkman leaving the gift of "life" on our doorsteps only to move on. In giving us life, he comes in to be with us and remain with us. Having once given life, then, he does not move on; he stays to make that life blossom and grow.[19]

16. The Joint Committee on Worship, *The Worshipbook* (Philadelphia: The Westminster Press, 1970), 220.
17. Ken Boa, *Conformed to His Image* (Grand Rapids: Zondervan, 2001), 292.
18. Boa, *Conformed to His Image*, 292.
19. Michael Reeves, *Delighting in the Trinity* (Downers Grove: IVP Academic, 2012), 90.

The Nature of the Holy Spirit

Some would see the Holy Spirit simply as an impersonal force in the universe. However, that is not the biblical perspective. The Holy Spirit is a person of the godhead and is referred to in Scripture by the personal pronoun "he" (John 14:15–17). In Scripture, the Holy Spirit carries out the will of God the Father, and he is the one who works in the lives of God's people to enable them to be all God intended.

The Holy Spirit reveals the following qualities:

Thought

The Holy Spirit has the capacity to think, to know and to understand the mind of God. The apostle Paul writes that the Spirit can "comprehend the thoughts of God" (1 Corinthians 2:11). The apostle John writes that the Holy Spirit would bring clarity to what Jesus had taught, as well as reminding God's people of the truth. "The Advocate, the Holy Spirit, whom the Father will send in my name, will teach you all things and will remind you of everything I have said to you" (John 14:26).

Emotion

Since the Holy Spirit is a person, he has all the emotional responses that a person does. Thus, he has all the emotions that we have as individuals. We can lie to the Spirit (Acts 5:3–5), we can grieve the Spirit (Ephesians 4:30), and we can even blaspheme against the Spirit (Matthew 12:31f), an act which will not be forgiven.

Will

The Holy Spirit is the one who acts decisively in the life of the believer to bring about God's plan. We see that he is the one who convicts us of sin (John 16:8), he empowers people to live a life that is pleasing to God (Romans 8:2–4, 11–14), and he is the one who determines the spiritual gifts that followers of Jesus will receive (1 Corinthians 12:11).

An Exercise

What character qualities of the Holy Spirit are indicated by the following descriptions? What do they indicate that one can gain by becoming more acquainted with the Holy Spirit?

Verse	Quality	Benefit
Isaiah 11:2		
John 14:17		
John 16:13–15		
Romans 8:2		
Romans 8:15–16		
1 Corinthians 2:2–5		
Ephesians 1:17		
2 Timothy 1:7		

Descriptions of the Holy Spirit

When we think about God the Father or Jesus the Son, these are concepts that are relatively easy to comprehend. However, when we speak about the Holy Spirit, this is a different matter. In the Bible, the images used for God the Holy Spirit are objects. The following five images or symbols reveal different aspects of the nature and work of the Holy Spirit.

Fire

Fire, particularly in the Old Testament, was a reference to the presence of God. For example, when God spoke to Moses, there was a bush that was on fire, but it was not consumed. Moses then realized he was standing on holy ground, and God spoke to him (Exodus 3:1–10). When the children of Israel were on the trek from Egypt to the Promised Land, there was a pillar of fire that hung in the sky at night to remind them that God was with them (Exodus 13:21). On the day of Pentecost, when the Holy Spirit descended upon the gathered followers of Jesus, there appeared tongues of fire that rested on each of them (Acts 2:3). There is also the reference to fire as being a part of the Holy Spirit's purifying power in the life of the believer and to bring judgment on the unbeliever (Luke 3:16–18).

Wind

Wind is a symbol that speaks of the invigorating power of the Holy Spirit to bring life. In the Old Testament, there are many such references to this work of the Spirit. Ezekiel the prophet had a vision of the wind blowing into the valley of dry bones, and as the wind passed over the bones, they came to life (Ezekiel 37:1–14). On the day of Pentecost, we are told that there was a mighty rushing wind filling the house as people were filled with the Holy Spirit (Acts 2:2–4). As these first followers of Jesus were empowered by the Holy Spirit, they were then sent out to minister in the name of Jesus.

Oil

In the Old Testament, oil was used as a sign that God was setting an individual apart for a special ministry or task and that they would be empowered for this task or ministry by the Spirit of God. David, the shepherd boy, was anointed by Samuel to be the next king of Israel after Saul's disastrous reign. We read: "Samuel took the horn of oil and anointed him in the presence of his brothers; and from that day on the Spirit of the LORD came upon David in power" (1 Samuel 16:13). In the New Testament, oil was used for medicinal purposes, as in the story of the Good Samaritan who put oil on the wounds of the man beaten by robbers (Luke 10:34). However, anointing with oil is also used in reference to prayer and healing (James 5:14–16).

Water

Water is a symbol that speaks of the regenerating power of the Holy Spirit. The prophet Ezekiel saw a stream of water that began as a trickle from the temple and made its way to the Dead Sea. Wherever the water went life began to spring up and flourish (Ezekiel 47:1–12). Jesus spoke about life-giving water in the life of a believer when he spoke with the woman at the well. He told her he would give her water that would become in her "a spring of water welling up to eternal life" (John 4:10–15). What Jesus was referencing was the fact that only the Spirit of God can satisfy the deepest needs of the human heart and bring life to every person.

Dove

When Jesus was baptized, we are told that the Spirit of God descended upon him as a dove from heaven. The dove is a symbol that represents gentleness and peace. In his ministry we see that Jesus treated people with a gentle touch, and his message was one of peace—peace with God and peace with one another (John 1:32–33).

The Divinity of the Holy Spirit

As we consider Scripture, we see that the Holy Spirit is not only associated with the Father and the Son but shares an equal place as part of the godhead. When Jesus gave final words of instruction to his disciples prior to his ascension, he instructed them to "go and make disciples of all nations, baptizing them in the name of the Father and of the Son and of the Holy Spirit" (Matthew 28:19).

Exercise

Note the following passages of Scripture. What do they indicate about the deity of the Holy Spirit?

Isaiah 40:13–14

Psalm 51:11

Acts 5:3–4

Hebrews 9:14

1 John 5:7

The Work of the Holy Spirit

In the Scriptures, there are many different aspects of the ministry of the Holy Spirit in the life of the individual and in the life of the church.

The Work of the Holy Spirit in the Individual

The Holy Spirit Convicts of Sin

The apostle John, conveying Jesus's words about the Holy Spirit, declares, "When he comes, he will prove the world to be in the wrong about sin and righteousness and judgment: about sin, because people do not believe in me; about righteousness, because the I am going to the Father, where you can see me no longer; and about judgment, because the prince of this world now stands condemned" (John 16:8–11). This is important to grasp because we cannot convince and convict people of their sin; this is the work of God's Spirit alone. He enables individuals to understand their true spiritual condition: they have sinned against a Holy God, they are under the judgment of God, and they need to appropriate the righteousness of Christ.

The Holy Spirit Brings About New Life

The Holy Spirit was active in creation (Genesis 1), and he is active in bringing about the new birth. When Jesus was approached by Nicodemus, a religious man, Jesus told him of the need to be "born of water and the Spirit" (John 3:4–6). Without the Spirit, there is no spiritual life. In fact, the only reason we respond to God is because the Holy Spirit has been working in our life, drawing us to God. This is the initial stage of becoming a Christian (John 3:3–5; 1 Thessalonians 2:13). Jesus spoke to Nicodemus about this new life. New Testament scholar Scott McKnight summarizes what it means to be born again or born anew. He states: "God's Spirit hovers over us and unleashes new creation into us. God's Spirit draws us to believe in Jesus, the Son of God. God's Spirit enters into those who are open to God in Christ. God's Spirit begins to transform us into Jesus followers."[20]

The Holy Spirit Lives in the Life of a Believer

When a person responds to God's invitation to new life, an amazing thing occurs. The apostle Paul describes it as "Christ making his home in our hearts." This means the Holy Spirit, who is the spirit of Jesus, lives within us. His dwelling in our life implies that he will empower us to live lives that are pleasing to God and to develop those qualities of life that are like the qualities exemplified by Jesus (Ephesians 3:16–17; Romans 8:9–11; Galatians 2:20; 5:22–23). McKnight points out, "If there is a secret to experiencing the fullness of the Christian life, it is this: we need the Spirit to empower us to live as God wants us to live. In fact, we cannot live the Christian life until we are open to the Spirit."[21]

The Holy Spirit Seeks to Make Christ Known

The ministry of the Holy Spirit is not to focus on himself but to reveal Christ in all his glory. It is Christ who is to control our lives. Therefore, we need to know who he is and what he desires if we are to live our lives in loving

20. McKnight, *Open to the Spirit*, 70.
21. McKnight, *Open to the Spirit*, 19.

obedience to him. This is accomplished by the work of the Spirit (John 15:26; 16:14; Acts 7:55). Author and minister David Watson states,

> It is always the work of the Spirit to exalt and magnify the Lord Jesus Christ. He will help Christians to honour Christ in their lives, to love and serve Christ in every way they can, to bear witness to Christ in an unbelieving world that is lost without him. He will reveal our completeness in Christ, the sovereignty of Christ, the finished work of Christ and the fact that God has blessed us with every spiritual blessing in Christ.[22]

The Work of the Holy Spirit in the Church

Unity

We are aware that in the Christian church there are many different denominations and traditions. This can be confusing to many who are outside the church. They wonder, if we are Christians, then why are there so many denominations? Furthermore, in some situations there can be disunity and conflict within local congregations. Again, people ask why. Are we not supposed to be united? Prior to his crucifixion and subsequent resurrection, Jesus prayed that his followers would be unified as one. Jesus declared, "I pray also for those who will believe in me … that all of them may be one, Father, just as you are in me and I am in you. May they also be in us so that the world may believe that you have sent me" (John 17:20–21).

How is this accomplished? It is accomplished by the work of the Holy Spirit. It is through him we are baptized into one faith. At conversion, we are brought into the life of the Spirit. This is true of all Christians who belong to the community of faith. Paul the apostle expresses it in these words: "There is one body and one Spirit, just as you were called to one hope when you were called; one Lord, one faith, one baptism; one God and Father of all, who is over all and through all and in all" (Ephesians 4:4–6). Thus, in relation to the church the Holy Spirit seeks to create unity, and at the same time it is our task to maintain that unity (Ephesians 4:3). At times this may be accomplished through bringing individuals who were at odds with each other into oneness through reconciliation (Ephesians 2:14–18).

---

22. David Watson, *One in the Spirit* (Toronto: Hodder and Stoughton, 1985), 36.

Unity is also accomplished by discovering the concept of Christian fellowship. In the early church this was demonstrated in different ways, such as sharing possessions, being in each other's homes, praying with and for each other, and worshipping together (Acts 2:42–47). The bottom line is that these Christians shared life together.

If there is a spirit of disunity or dissension within the church, we need to repent and ask the Spirit of God to empower us to live together in unity. This is the will of God!

Diversity

Although we pray for unity, there is a place for diversity. The Holy Spirit has given different spiritual gifts, as he determines, to each believer. These gifts recognize the uniqueness of each person and at the same time they are to be used in the context of the community of faith for the mutual building up of each person in their faith (1 Corinthians 12:1–11; Ephesians 4:11–16).

The church, which is the body of believers, is made up of many different people who have different spiritual gifts. The apostle Paul compares it to the human body with different parts, and each part is essential for the functioning of the body. Therefore, it is important that everyone in the church with their different spiritual gifts see themselves as significant parts of the whole body. It is in this context we minister to each other.

We have different gifts, and we are to minister to each other, but what is the purpose of these gifts? The goal or purpose in all of this is to build up the people of God to the place of spiritual maturity. As we live together in unity, and as we minister to each other with our different spiritual gifts, the church will make a great impact on the culture simply because we are cooperating with the Spirit of God.

McKnight emphasizes three essential factors about the spiritual gifts. One, they are given by God. Two, every Christian is granted one or more gifts. Three, gifts are given for the common good. He states,

> We are not given gifts so we grow personally, though we will grow in learning how to use our gifts. We are not given gifts so we can be known for our gifts. Instead, we are given gifts for the good of the church, and by this Paul meant primarily the good of our local church's ministries. When we become open to the Spirit, we receive an entirely new orientation in life.[23]

23. McKnight, *Open to the Spirit*, 117.

The following passages list some of the spiritual gifts that the Spirit gives to individuals: Romans 12:6–8, 1 Corinthians 12:8–10, Ephesians 4:11–12, and 1 Peter 4:1.

DISCUSSION QUESTIONS ABOUT THE PERSON AND WORK OF THE HOLY SPIRIT

The Holy Spirit, sometimes referred to as the "forgotten person of the Trinity," is often misunderstood. The following questions will give you more insight into his person and work.

Read John 16:8–16.

4–1. How would you paraphrase the three goals of the work of the Holy Spirt?

Jesus declared it was good that he should leave. What do you understand him to mean by that? How is it good? Would you not want him to be present? Explain your answer.

Of the different roles that the Holy Spirit is engaged in, which ones have you experienced in your life?

Read Romans 8:1–17.

4–2. In verses 1–4, the writer references living according to the Spirit. Read verses 5–11, and make a list of what it means to walk according to a sinful nature and according to the Spirit.

How can we learn to be led by the Spirit (v. 14)?

Verses 14–17 imply we can have an intimate relationship with God and know we are the children of God. What does that mean to you?

Can you recall any example of how the Holy Spirit is enabling you to "put to death the misdeeds of the body"?

Read Galatians 5:16–26.

4–3. In this passage, you will discover that life in the Spirit is very positive in contrast to life that is controlled by our sinful nature. Note the extreme contrast in lifestyle.

4–4. If the Holy Spirit abides in our life and has given us "new life," why do we still struggle with sin?

4–5. What does it mean, in verse 24, that we have "crucified the flesh with its passions and desires"? How does one do that?

4–6. As you explore the nine characteristics of the fruit of the Spirit, which one(s) have you noticed to be developing in your life? How does that happen?

4–7. Is there one "fruit" that you would like to see develop in this season of your life?

Read Philippians 2:12–13.

4–8. If the Christian life is governed by the Holy Spirit, what is your responsibility in living out your relationship with God? Explain what you would do.

5.
THE CROSS

Introduction

Many symbols have been used to depict significant features of the Christian faith, such as a dove, fire, or fish. However, since the second century, the cross has been the pictorial symbol that universally speaks of the saving work of Jesus Christ, who died on a cross to pay the penalty for sin. This symbol is affixed to church buildings, worn as jewelry, and marked on themselves or on others by many Christians, such as when entering a church or on their foreheads on Ash Wednesday. All of this serves as a reminder of Jesus's saving work for humankind.

The Cross Is Central to Christianity

The Bible depicts the cross as the essence of Jesus's life and mission. In other words, everything about the life of Jesus is focused on the cross and what it means. This is the centrepiece of the Christian faith.

In foretelling the birth of Jesus, the angel told Joseph that this child would "save his people from their sins" (Matthew 1:21).

Even as a young boy of twelve when he was at the temple sitting among the teachers, Jesus was aware that the Father has sent him into the world to fulfill a mission (Luke 2:41–52). There are three incidents that predicted his mission, as recorded in the Gospel of Mark.

The first incident occurred as Jesus entered Caesarea Philippi, a city known for its inclusivity of various religious traditions. Here Jesus asked his disciples who people thought he was. Although the general consensus was that Jesus was one of the great prophets, Peter replied that Jesus was the Messiah. Jesus explained that as the Messiah he must suffer and die. Peter was horrified! (Mark 8:27–33).

The second incident occurred after Jesus healed a little boy who had an impure spirit that caused him to suffer greatly. Jesus and the disciples left that place, and when they were alone Jesus told them he would be delivered into the hands of men; they would put him to death, and on the third day he would rise from death. Although the disciples heard what Jesus was saying, they simply did not understand what it meant (Mark 9:14–32).

The third incident occurred as Jesus and the disciples were making their way to Jerusalem. Along the way Jesus told the disciples, in detail, that in Jerusalem he would be handed over to various officials and they would take his life. However, on the third day he would rise from the dead (Mark 10:32–34).

The Necessity of the Cross

Why is the cross so significant in the Christian faith? To understand the significance of the cross, we must grasp its importance in the light of our relationship with God.

God created people so that they could be in fellowship with him. From the beginning of creation, our first ancestors, Adam and Eve, had an intimate relationship with God and in that context, they were free to make choices. God told them they had access to everything in the garden, with one exception. They were not to eat of the tree of the knowledge of good and evil. They could choose to obey or disobey God (Genesis 2; Genesis 3:6–7). Either way, they would live with the consequences.

Freedom is an essential aspect of our humanity, but at the same time we must accept responsibility for the decisions we make. In the story of the fall of humanity, we see two individuals who made choices that led to serious consequences. Adam and Eve decided to disobey God's directive. The consequence of this decision and action brought sin into the world, and as a result death entered the human race (Genesis 3). The intimacy God intended for us to have with him was gone, and we were separated from God.

Since God intended humankind to live in relationship with one another on a collective basis, it is not surprising that Scripture teaches that the whole human race is now subject to the consequences of the fall.

The result of the original sin of Adam and Eve is that we are now separated from God. This is spiritual death. This is God's judgment upon sin and there is nothing we can do to remedy this reality. Faced with this judgment, the Scriptures make it clear that God alone can save us and restore the relationship (Romans 6:23).

The Purpose of Christ's Death

People separated and estranged from God need to be restored to the relationship that God originally intended. Since we can't do anything to restore the relationship, we are totally dependent on God to do so.

Therefore, Jesus came into the world to rescue us from our sin, to pay the penalty we deserve, and to restore us to God.

This act of restoration was accomplished by Jesus, who sacrificed his life by paying the debt we owe for our sins and dying in our place. This act is known as the *atonement*. The Scriptures are clear that God, by virtue of his holy nature, cannot overlook sin but must bring punishment to bear upon it. The psalmist writes, "You are not a God who is pleased with wickedness; with you, evil people are not welcome. The arrogant cannot stand in your presence. You hate all who do wrong" (Psalm 5:4–5).

The apostle Paul writes: "The wrath of God is being revealed from heaven against all the godlessness and wickedness of people, who suppress the truth by their wickedness" (Romans 1:18).

Jesus's death on the cross for the sins of others is called a *vicarious sacrifice*. This implies that someone else took the place of the sinner and bore the judgment and punishment they deserved.

The concept of vicarious sacrifice has its origin in the Old Testament. The Israelites would bring a sacrifice to offer to God. People would lay their hands on the animal to be sacrificed and confess their sins. This action symbolized the transfer of their sin to the animal to be sacrificed.

In the New Testament, we read that Jesus is the one who offered his life as a sacrifice for the sins of others. The guilt and punishment of sinners was transferred to him. There are several passages in Scripture that refer to our sins being "laid upon" Christ. The most familiar passage is from the prophet Isaiah, who wrote: "Surely he took up our pain and bore our suffering, yet we considered him punished by God, stricken by him, and afflicted. But he was pierced for our transgressions, he was crushed for our iniquities; the punishment that brought us peace was on him, and by his wounds we are healed" (Isaiah 53:4–5).

Noted author and Bible expositor John Stott declared that the sacrificial death of Jesus on the cross is the heart of the Christian gospel, and that it enforces the following three truths about God, Jesus Christ, and us:

> Our sin must be extremely horrible.
> God's love must be beyond comprehension.
> Christ's salvation must be a free gift.[24]

What the Cross Accomplished

As a result of the death of Jesus, our sins can be forgiven, we are accepted by God, and he makes us into new people. The apostle Paul writes: "If anyone is in Christ, the new creation has come. The old has gone and the new is here! All this is from God, who reconciled us to himself through Christ" (2 Corinthians 5:17–18).

There are three theological concepts that help explain this.

Redemption

The most basic understanding of *redeem* is "to buy back." In the Old Testament, people were redeemed from various situations, such as slavery, debt, or exile. Spiritually speaking, we are in moral bondage as a result of our sins, and Christ has redeemed us. Mark, in his Gospel, quotes Jesus: "The Son of Man did not come to be served, but to serve, and to give his life as a ransom for many" (Mark 10:45).

The second factor to consider regarding our redemption is the price that was paid. The most common term used in the New Testament refers to the *blood* of Christ. This term is steeped in sacrificial imagery, which refers to the sacrificial death of Jesus on the cross. The apostle Peter makes reference to this truth: "You know that it was not with perishable things such as silver or gold that you were redeemed from the empty way of life handed down to you from your ancestors, but with the precious blood of Christ, a lamb without blemish or defect" (1 Peter 1:18–19).

We have been bought (redeemed) by Christ's sacrificial death, and now we belong to him, and we are to live for him. The apostle Paul says, "Do you not know that your bodies are temples of the Holy Spirit, who is in you, whom

24. J. R. W. Stott, *The Cross of Christ* (Downers Grove: InterVarsity Press, 1986), 83.

you have received from God? You are not your own; you were bought at a price. Therefore honour God with your bodies" (1 Corinthians 6:19–20).

Justification

Justification is one of the key words in understanding our salvation. The word basically means that God declares us to be righteous. However, there are several aspects of justification that need to be considered.

John Stott, mentioned earlier, explores four key phrases that elaborate on this concept of justification. He writes that the source of our justification is by God's grace.[25] This means that justification is God's favour shown toward us. The apostle Paul encourages us: "If God is for us, who can be against us? ... Who will bring any charge against those whom God has chosen? It is God who justifies" (Romans 8:31–33).

Second, we are justified by Christ's blood. This is the ground of our salvation. Stott states,

> When God justifies sinners, he is not declaring bad people good or saying they are not sinners after all; he is pronouncing them legally righteous, free from any liability to the broken law, because he himself in his Son has borne the penalty of their law breaking ... In other words we are justified by his blood. There could be no justification without atonement.[26]

Third, we are justified by faith. This means we have absolutely nothing to do with our standing before God. There is no place for thinking that our good deeds can outweigh our bad deeds and that somehow we can be acceptable before God. We simply trust in the atoning work of Christ alone to be forgiven of our sins.[27]

Fourth, we are justified in Christ. This points to the relationship we have with him at the present moment. We belong to Christ, and by extension we belong to one another, the community of faith—the church (Galatians 3:26–29).[28]

----

25. Stott, *The Cross of Christ*, 189.
26. Stott, *The Cross of Christ*, 190.
27. Stott, *The Cross of Christ*, 190.
28. Stott, *The Cross of Christ*, 191.

Reconciliation

Reconciliation is a very positive concept. It refers to the fact that though we were once alienated from God, that relationship has been restored, and we are now reconciled. Consequently, we are able to be in the type of relationship God intended from the beginning with Adam and Eve in the garden of Eden. Paul writes,

> If, when we were God's enemies, we were reconciled to him through the death of his Son, how much more, having been reconciled, shall we be saved through his life! Not only is this so, but we also boast in God through our Lord Jesus Christ, through whom we have now received reconciliation. (Romans 5:10–11)

But there is more to being reconciled with God. It means we have a new status with God, being adopted into his family. We are no longer considered slaves, but children of God and heirs with Christ (Romans 8:14–17; Galatians 3:26–29). Being children of God, who is our heavenly Father, means we have complete access to God, anytime, anywhere.

DISCUSSION QUESTIONS ABOUT THE MEANING AND PURPOSE OF THE CROSS

The cross of Christ is central to the Christian faith. The Bible teaches that humankind is estranged from God and that by our efforts we are not able to restore the relationship. Thus, Jesus died on the cross to pay the penalty for our sins and give us the gift of eternal life. This gift is available to all who will receive it. It is life-changing!

Read Ecclesiastes 2:1–11.

> 5–1. How would you describe this person's life? Why does this person seem to be so unhappy with what many would describe as a very successful life?

What do you think about living such a life without God?

Read Romans 3:9–26.

5–2. There are many who think they are good people. What do verses 10–18 tell us about who we are?

What is our perspective toward God?

5–3. What do the terms *justification*, *atonement*, and *redemption* mean?

5–4. How do you apply these terms to the death of Christ and the implications for your life?

Read Romans 5:6–11.

5–5. How does the death of Christ impact your relationship with God?

Read 1 John 5:11–12.

5–6. What security do you have in your relationship with God? How do you know it to be true?

Read 1 John 1:8–9.

5–7. The reality is, we will continue to sin, and this can break our relationship with God. How can you keep this relationship alive and dynamic?

Read 2 Peter 1:3–11.

5–8. It is important that our relationship with God grow and mature. Effort is required on our part if that is to happen. What is stated explicitly in this passage? What are the positive results?

Read Romans 8:1–2, 28–39.

5–9. How does this passage give you confidence as you continue the journey through life?

Will this change the way you look at life each day? Explain.

Steps to Beginning a Relationship with God[29]

God's Purpose

God desires to have a relationship with you so that you can have life that is full and life that is eternal.

"I have come that they may have life, and have it to the full." —Jesus (John 10:10)

"For God so loved the world that he gave his one and only Son, that whoever believes in him shall not perish but have eternal life." —Jesus (John 3:16)

Why do most not experience this?

---

29. Adapted from *Peace with God*, used by permission the Billy Graham Evangelistic Association.

Our Problem

God created humankind in his image and likeness to have abundant life. However, he did not make us robots to automatically love and obey him. God gave us a will and freedom of choice. Sadly, we chose to go against God's commands. The result of that decision was separation from God, and we must live with the consequences.

> All have sinned and fall short of the glory of God. (Romans 3:23)

> The wages of sin is death, but the gift of God is eternal life in Christ Jesus our Lord. (Romans 6:23)

No matter how hard we try, all our efforts will not be good enough to restore the brokenness in this relationship.

> There is a way that appears to be right, but in the end it leads to death. (Proverbs 14:12)

God's Intervention—The Cross

When Jesus died on the cross, he paid the penalty for your sins. Only he could do that since he alone is the sinless one. As forgiven people, we can have access to God, our heavenly Father.

> Christ … suffered once for sins, the righteous for the unrighteous, to bring you to God. (1 Peter 3:18)

> God demonstrates his own love for us in this: While we were still sinners, Christ died for us. (Romans 5:8)

If that is what Christ did for us, we must make a choice.

My Response

Will I receive the gift of God's forgiveness available only through his Son, Jesus Christ?

Yet to all who did receive him, to those who believed in his name, he gave the right to become children of God. (John 1:12)

If you declare with your mouth, "Jesus is Lord," and believe in your heart that God raised him from the dead, you will be saved. (Romans 10:9)

God's Assurance

Everyone who calls on the name of the Lord will be saved. (Romans 10:13)

For it is by grace you have been saved, through faith—and this is the not from yourselves, it is the gift of God—not by works, so that no one can boast. (Ephesians 2:8–9)

Receiving Christ, we are born into God's family through the supernatural work of the Holy Spirit who indwells every believer. This is called regeneration or the new birth.

6.
THE CHURCH

Introduction

God created us as individual beings, therefore we need to understand that we thrive best when we are in community. This has been expressed very succinctly as "better together."

In our Western world, we have emphasized the autonomy, independence, and self determination of the individual. All of this has led to superficial relationships and many lonely people.

This is not what God intends for his people. Theologian Ken Boa states, "We come to faith as individuals, but we grow in community. Life in Jesus is not meant to be solitary and individualistic, but shared and collective."[30] In fact, Boa argues that "the nature of the community of faith is designed to prepare us for our everlasting life with the Lord and with one another."[31] In essence, he is stating what Scripture teaches: namely, the church is important for our life together.

At the same time, we recognize that no church is perfect and that many people have been wounded and hurt by church leaders and congregations. The solitary Christian is an unknown entity in the New Testament. The apostle Paul writes, "We were all baptised by one Spirit so as to form one body" (1 Corinthians 12:13). McKnight states, "We weren't baptized in the Spirit to form our own brand of spirituality apart from the fellowship of other Christians."[32]

---

30. Ken Boa, *Conformed to His Image*, 416.
31. Boa, *Conformed to His Image*, 416
32. McKnight, *Open to the Spirit*, 104.

The idea of church has different connotations for different people. Most tend to think of church as a designation for a certain building in a specific location that is used for religious purposes. Others might think the term refers to a specific denomination, such as Presbyterian, Baptist, Methodist, or Pentecostal.

In the New Testament, the most common Greek word that refers to the church is *ekklesia* from the two Greek words *ek* and *kaleo*, which means to "call out." Therefore, the term *ekklesia* refers to the "called out" people of God. Since it is God who calls us to be a special people, we recognize his calling of a people is an act of his sovereign choice, and this choice is simply based on the reality that God has chosen to love us.

A prefigure of the church was the calling of the nation of Israel to be God's people. In choosing them, Moses spoke to the nation of Israel and declared,

> You are a people holy to the Lord our God. The Lord your God has chosen you out of all the peoples on the face of the earth to be his people, his treasured possession. The Lord did not set his affection on you and choose you because you were more numerous than other peoples, for you were the fewest of all peoples. But it was because the Lord loved you and kept the oath he swore to your ancestors that he brought you out with a mighty hand and redeemed you from the land of slavery. (Deuteronomy 7:6–8)

The Nature of the Church

It is important to realize that the church is composed of people who love and seek to follow God. In one of the great creeds (statements of belief) of the church, known as the Apostles' Creed, which is held by all Christians, we boldly state: "I believe in one holy, catholic [universal] and apostolic church." Commenting on this statement, theologian J. I. Packer states, "It is holy because it is consecrated to God; it is catholic because it embraces all Christians everywhere; and it is apostolic because it seeks to maintain the apostles's doctrine."[33]

The Church Universal

The church of Jesus Christ is composed of people from every race and nation on the earth. People from every era of history with different levels of spiritual maturity, from a mature believer to a recent convert to Christ, are part

33. Packer, *I Want to Be a Christian*, 85.

of the church. The apostle Paul, writing to the church in Colossae, declares that we are all one in Christ: "Here [in Christ] there is no Gentile or Jew, circumcised or uncircumcised, barbarian, Scythian, slave or free, but Christ is all, and is in all" (Colossians 3:11).

The Church Local and Visible

Even though the church is universal, there is also a local gathering where Christians meet. This is evident from the very beginning, when the early church was formed. Luke, writing about the young church, relates four things that they did together: "They devoted themselves to the apostles' teaching and to the fellowship, to the breaking of bread and to prayer" (Acts 2:42).

These young Christians learned the necessity of life together so that they could give and receive help in developing their spiritual life and gifts. Together they offered their acts of worship with one voice and with one heart. The concept of the solitary Christian was foreign to the early church. Community was of the essence.

The Church Invisible

The church invisible refers to all who have professed faith in Jesus as Lord. This includes all people throughout history. However, it is important to realize that all who are part of the church invisible ought to be an integral part of the church local and visible. On the other hand, simply being a member of the church local and visible does not necessarily mean that they belong to the church invisible.

You may have your name on a baptismal register or be a member of a congregation and yet not have your name written in the Lamb's Book of Life. In other words, you may not belong to Christ. At the final judgment, when all shall stand before God at the great white throne, it is essential that your name be written in the Book of Life (Revelation 20:11–15).

Description of the Church

The Family of God

The term *family* indicates a relationship with God as our heavenly Father, who is the head of the family, and with other members of the household. In this relationship, there is no room for segregation or other barriers that society might erect, such as political, social, educational, economic, or racial. The apostle Paul, in his letter to the Christians in Ephesus, describes them as members of "God's household" (Ephesians 2:19). As with most families, there will be some differences and at times not everyone will get along. However, we need to remember that we have one Father, and in the family of God we are all brothers and sisters. Therefore, it is important that we learn to get along with each other. This is something we need to work at constantly (Psalm 133; Ephesians 4:1–6).

The Bride of Christ

The phrase *bride of Christ* is an analogy that describes the intimacy God desires to have with his people, the church. We, as the bride of Christ, are to have a relationship with Christ that is marked by faithfulness and devotion to him. Christ loves the church with a pure and holy love, and he calls us to respond to that love by our commitment to be faithful to him, and to him alone.

The apostle Paul, writing to the church, provides a detailed description of how husbands and wives ought to relate to one another. After some instructions, he concludes by stating that this relationship is a mystery and that he is talking about Christ and the church. He says, "Each one of you also must love his wife as he loves himself, and the wife must respect her husband" (Ephesians 5:33).

All of this speaks to the fact we are to be committed in our devotion to Christ.

The Temple of God

This analogy comes from the Old Testament reference to the temple, which was the focus of Israel's worship. In this era the worship of Israel was very tangible with an emphasis on sacrifices and the observance of special days.

Jesus indicated the time was coming when true worshippers would worship God in spirit and in truth (John 4:23). No longer would people need a building to worship God; instead, they would be made a holy temple by the indwelling of the Holy Spirit. Thus, a building is no longer the house of God; rather, God's people are a temple.

There are several unique features about this building.

1. Christ is the architect (Matthew 16:18).
2. Christ is the foundation (1 Corinthians 3:11).
3. People or believers are called "living stones" (1 Peter 2:5).

The Body of Christ

The phrase *body of Christ* is perhaps the most familiar metaphor of the church. This metaphor expresses not only the relationship between Christ and the church but also the relationship between the various members of the church. This concept portrays the church as an organic unity in which all Christians not only belong to Christ but also to one another.

If the church is to grow and mature as a body, then there are several things that must occur. The body must be united in love and recognize that unity is essential (1 Corinthians 12:12–20). The body is equipped for ministry (Ephesians 4:11–13). There is the discovery, development, and utilization of spiritual gifts (Romans 12:3–8; 1 Corinthians 12; Ephesians 4:1–16).

The Mission of the Church

Everyone who is a member of the church needs to understand God's purpose for the church and to be wholeheartedly engaged in God's mission. There are four aspects of that mission: worship, evangelism, service, and maintaining truth.

Worship

The church is a worshipping community. One of the great dangers is to believe that we are to be engaged first and foremost in evangelism and mission. As important as they are, the church will be ineffective if we do not make worship the priority of our life, for we will virtually have nothing that is lasting to offer to God and will be ineffective. In worship, we focus on God, who he is, our relationship with him, and that he alone is the one who is worthy of all praise and adoration.

Our worship depends on three essential factors:

Worship must be directed toward God (Psalm 34:3).

Worship must be done in the power of the Holy Spirit (John 4: 23).

Worship ought to incorporate the body of Christ. There is a place for personal worship and a place for corporate worship. There are various accounts in the book of Acts of the church gathered in prayer and worship (Acts 2:1–4; 42–47).

Evangelism

Before he ascended to heaven, Jesus gave his followers a command to go into the world and make disciples of all people. This command has not been rescinded and is to be carried out in every generation. The message we are to proclaim is that the forgiveness of sins and the gift of God's Spirit are for all who repent of their sins and trust Christ as their Saviour and Lord (Matthew 28:18–20).

Service

The church is called not only to proclaim the good news of Jesus's love and forgiveness but also to live out, within the context of the culture, the concern of God for the whole person. We are called to feed the hungry, care for the sick, visit those in prison, seek justice, and advocate for those marginalised by society. Jesus continually modelled this type of lifestyle, and as his followers we are to do the same (Matthew 25:34–36; 1 John 3:17–18; Titus 3:8).

Maintain the Truth

In the Scriptures, God has revealed the truth about himself. The task of the church is to teach the truth about God as revealed in Scripture so that the church might pattern its life on that basis alone.

It is on the basis of Scripture that we continually challenge any teaching that is contrary to the truth as revealed in Scripture. At the same time, the church must recognize the presence and power of evil so that it will not overcome the power of good. The church must continually challenge evil by its determination to live and teach the truth.

The document *Living Faith* succinctly describes the purpose of the Scriptures as it relates to life:

> The Bible has been given to us by the inspiration of God to be the rule of faith and life. It is the standard of all doctrine by which we must test any word that comes to us from church, world or experience. We subject to its judgments all we believe and do. Through the Scriptures the church is bound only to Jesus Christ its King and Head. He is the living Word of God to whom the written word bears witness.[34]

DISCUSSION QUESTIONS ABOUT THE NATURE OF THE CHURCH

The church is not a building; rather, it is the whole people of God, called to share in the ministry of Christ in the world.

The questions in this study are designed to help you explore your understanding of the church and your role in it.

Being a part of a local assembly of believers is the norm in the New Testament. John Wesley is credited with saying: "The Bible knows nothing of solitary religion."

Read Acts 2:42–47.

6–1. How would you describe the life these people experienced?

---

34. The Presbyterian Church in Canada, *Living Faith: A Statement of Christian Belief* (Winfield: Wood Lake Books, 1984), 14.

What are the main features of their life together?

How would this compare with what you have experienced in a local congregation? Are there things you would like to change?

Read Hebrews 10:19–24.

6–2. In this passage, there are three statements that begin with "let us." Why do you think the author needed to address these issues? Do you see their relevance and need in the church today? Explain.

Read 1 Peter 2:4–10.

6–3. How are followers of Jesus described in this passage? When you read these descriptions, what do you think and feel? Do you find it challenging to live this out?

Read Ephesians 4:1–6.

6–4. Even though we are described as the family of God, at times it is not easy to get along with each other. All families struggle with this. What are the qualities that ought to characterise the community of faith? Describe them in practical terms.

In what way do you think grasping the truth that God is our Father will help you to live with one another?

Read Matthew 25:31–45.

6–5. Consider this statement, "The church exists primarily for the sake of those who are still outside it" (William Temple, English theologian and archbishop, 1881–1944).

What does this passage teach you about our responsibility to others as followers of Jesus? How does this challenge you? What practical steps could one take to fulfill this mandate?

7.
BAPTISM

Introduction

Before we consider baptism and the Lord's Supper, we want to have a general understanding about their significance. Many churches refer to them as sacraments, other churches use the term ordinances. Sacraments are not simply pledges or acts of dedication of our life to God, rather they are actually the means that God uses to bless us. Since they are important practices of the church that confesses Jesus as Lord, it is important to understand why they are so significant.

These practices have not developed over the course of church history. Rather, they were instituted by Christ himself. In the Protestant church, we believe that two sacraments were given to us by Christ: baptism and the Lord's Supper. In the Eastern Church, they were called mysteries, implying disclosure of that which was previously hidden. In the Western Church, they were referred to as sacraments, implying solemn pledges.[35]

These sacraments act as a visible sign of Christ's redeeming work for us, and they are a seal of the covenant of grace. In ancient days, a royal document had a seal placed on it, signifying its authenticity. The sacraments are a seal on our life, signifying that we belong to Christ as his own.

The physical signs for baptism (water) and the Lord's Supper (bread and wine) represent our spiritual relationship with Christ. Baptism signifies the washing away of our sins, and the Lord's Supper signifies our communion with God and with one another. These sacraments are not in and of themselves the means of our salvation; rather, they serve to nourish and sustain our faith. The act of being baptised with water or the act of eating bread and drinking wine at the Lord's Supper are nothing in themselves. However, when the Holy Spirit works though these elements and in the life of the believer, the person is renewed and has communion with Christ.

---

35. Packer, *I Want to Be a Christian*, 118.

It needs to be acknowledged that there are different interpretations about the meaning of the sacraments and at times this has caused bitter controversy and conflict in the church. In this study, we examine the issues from a broad biblical basis.

Baptism

Baptism is seen as the visible sign of entrance or initiation in the Christian church. The word *baptise* comes from the Greek *baptizo*, meaning, in its most literal sense, to dip. This action would suggest both washing and cleansing.

There are some different images of baptism presented in the Bible:

> Washing (1 Corinthians 6:11)
> Putting on new clothes (Galatians 3:27)
> Coming to life from death (Romans 6:4)

Biblical scholar N. T. Wright states that baptism has a powerful implication for one who has been baptised. He contends that the apostle Paul viewed baptism, as he explained in Romans 6, as "someone who had been baptized into the Messiah had already died, been buried, and had been raised to new life. That had happened to Jesus, and what was true of him was true of his people."[36]

Is Baptism Necessary?

This is a question that many people ask, and some would suggest that what is important is to simply confess Christ as Lord. As significant as that confession is, the teaching of Scripture is very clear. First and foremost, Jesus gave a mandate to the church: "Go and make disciples of all nations, baptising them in the name of the Father and of the Son and of the Holy Spirit" (see Matthew 28:18–20). Therefore, if we acknowledge him as Lord of our life, we are to be obedient to his commands.

Second, baptism is the mark of belonging to the church. John Calvin, a revered 16th century theologian and reformer, defined baptism, in his *Institutes of Religion*, as "the sign of initiation by which we are received into the

36. N. T. Wright, *The Day the Revolution Began* (New York: HarperOne, 2016), 378.

society of the church, in order that, engrafted in Christ, we may be reckoned among God's children."[37] On the day of Pentecost, not only were people being saved, but they were being added to the church. On that day three thousand were baptised (Acts 2:38, 41, 47).

Third, it is important to understand that baptism is more than a witness to our conversion. Author Michael Green states, "In the New Testament [baptism] is much more clearly identified as an instrument of conversion."[38]

Through baptism you are saved (1 Peter 3:21).

Through baptism you are buried and raised to new life in Christ (Romans 6:3–4).

Through baptism you are incorporated into the body of Christ (1 Corinthians 12:13).

The Meaning of Baptism

There are several meanings associated with baptism.

Washing/Cleansing

Washing describes an action whereby dirt is removed, and the person becomes clean. From a spiritual perspective, this washing implies that our sin and guilt are removed. It is washed away, and we stand before God with a clean heart.

The apostle Paul, standing before a crowd of people while preaching at the temple, was arrested and then taken to a military barracks. Before entering the barracks, he asked for permission to speak. He told of his conversion experience on the Damascus Road and then he pleaded with the people, "Get up, be baptised and wash your sins away, calling on his name" (Acts 22:16).

---

37. Dennis Okholm, "A Reformed Theology of Baptism" in *Sacred Actions of Christian Worship*, vol. IV, ed. Robert Webber (Nashville: Star Song, 1994), 132.
38. Michael Green, *Baptism* (Downers Grove: Intervarsity Press, 1987), 61

Union with Christ

A second aspect of our baptism emphasizes that our life is now united with Christ's. We are baptised into Christ, and this act declares that before God we are justified in his sight. Paul, writing to the Galatians, expresses it like this: "I no longer live, but Christ lives in me. The life I now live in the body, I live by faith in the Son of God, who loved me and gave himself for me" (Galatians 2:20).

A corollary to our union with Christ is that we are not only united with him, but we are also united with one another in the body of Christ. In describing the unity of the church, Paul states that though we are quite different as people and we have different spiritual gifts that unite us, "we are all baptised by one Spirit so as to form one body" (1 Corinthians 12:13).

The Baptismal Formula

The apostles were instructed to baptize "in the name of the Father and of the Son and of the Holy Spirit" (Matthew 28:19).

This formula is understood to imply that the person being baptized is being placed in a special relationship with God as characterized by God's revelation of himself through his names.

There is a reference in the New Testament of people being baptised in the name of Jesus (Acts 2:38). This may refer to the confession that Jesus is the Messiah, and on the basis of that confession people were baptised.

The Mode of Baptism

Most within the Christian church do not place any special emphasis upon a particular mode of baptism with the exception of certain groups, such as Baptists. There does not seem to be any one mode of baptism being described in the biblical accounts. However, based on early historical accounts, immersion was the most common form of baptism in the early church.

However, it is unwarranted to claim that "to baptise" always implies immersion. The verb *to baptise* can mean "to wash," "to bathe," or "to purify by washing." Sometimes this purification occurred by "sprinkling." When the religious leaders of Judaism would return to their homes, they would sprinkle water, as an act of purification, on different parts of their body and on articles in their homes. The Greek verb used to describe this purification when translated into English means "to baptise" (Mark 7:3–4). It would be rather odd to fully immerse their bodies or household articles to complete the ritual of purification.

There are records of baptisms where the circumstances would probably not permit baptism by immersion.

Two examples to consider:

- The baptism of three thousand in Jerusalem in one day (Acts 2:41). Would immersion be the method?

- The baptism of the Philippian jailer and his household (Acts 16:33). This occurred late at night.

In essence, all methods of baptism are valid, whether by immersion, pouring, or sprinkling. What we need to keep first and foremost in our minds is the meaning of baptism.

Who Can Be Baptised?

There are two categories of candidates for baptism.

Adults

In the New Testament, it is evident that adult believers were baptised when they professed faith in Christ. Usually, the baptism was done immediately. On the day of Pentecost, Peter, preaching to the crowd, declared,

> "Repent and be baptised, every one of you, in the name of Jesus Christ for the forgiveness of sins." … With many other words he warned them; and he pleaded with them … Those who accepted his message were baptised, and about three thousand were added to their number that day. (Acts 2:38–41)

In the case of adults being baptised, the church has always insisted they make a credible profession of faith. Theologian Louis Berkhof states, "This profession of faith presupposes regeneration, faith, conversion and justification."[39]

Since the early church was a missionary church, it is realistic to assume that most converts were adults who were capable of making a credible profession of faith. Today in the church, as we celebrate adult baptism, all we can do is accept at face value the profession of faith, unless there is valid reason to doubt the sincerity of such a profession.

Infants

The baptism of infants of believing parents, though it is practiced by many Christian churches, is not accepted by all.

At the outset it needs to be stated that the Bible neither commands nor forbids the baptism of infants. However, this does not mean the baptism of infants is unwarranted. The practice of infant baptism is linked with the covenant.

In the Old Testament, male circumcision, the outward sign of the covenant, was done simply because God commanded it to be done. This was an act whereby the parents claimed God's covenant promises for their child, and the sign was given. Thus, a child born into the home of believers had the right to the sign of belonging even though the child was too young to fulfill the conditions. As children grew into adulthood, they could then embrace or renounce the covenant.

Those who support infant baptism argue that the covenant has not changed. There is only one covenant, but what has changed is the sign of the covenant. In the Old Testament the sign was circumcision.

God said to Abraham,

> "As for you, you must keep my covenant, you and your descendants after you for the generations to come … This is my covenant with you…: Every male among you shall be circumcised … It will be the sign of the covenant between me and you … My covenant in your flesh is to be an everlasting covenant." (Genesis 17:9–13)

---

39. Berkhof, *Systematic Theology*, 632.

In the New Testament, the sign of the covenant is not circumcision but baptism. The apostle Paul helps us understand that baptism is the new sign available to all who are in Christ.

> In him [Christ] you were also circumcised with a circumcision not performed by human hands. Your whole self ruled by the flesh was put off when you were circumcised by Christ, having been buried with him in baptism, in which you were also raised with him through your faith in the working of God, who raised him from the dead. (Colossians 2:11–12)

In both the Old and New Testaments, the parents of the child are claiming God's covenant promise for their child until that time when the individual personally affirms the covenant. In fact, Paul goes so far as to state that under the new covenant the believer's children are made holy (1 Corinthians 7:14).

Theologian J. I. Packer states, "If parent-child solidarity under God's covenant is an unchanging fact on which was based God's former command of circumcision, the then covenant sign for baby boys, how can it be proper to deny baptism, the new covenant sign, to babies now?"[40]

Some will argue that baptism does not replace circumcision. But if it does not, then there is no other initiatory rite mentioned in the New Testament.

There is also the argument that infant baptism was practiced in the early church, as there are several examples of household baptism. In that culture, when the head of the household was converted, that individual and all members of the household were baptised. Paul and Silas saw this happen with the Philippian jailer, who was converted under their ministry, and immediately "he and his household were baptised" (Acts 16:33). It's hard to believe that households would not include infants and young children (1 Corinthians 1:16).

However, those who practice infant baptism would emphasize that one does not baptise infants indiscriminately. This rite belongs only to parents who are believers, and these parents must give evidence of a credible faith. If they don't believe, how can they claim God's promises for their child?

---

40. Packer, *I Want to Be a Christian*, 145.

Confirmation

It is important that each person make a public confession of faith. When we baptise children, we anticipate the day when the child declares "Jesus is Lord." The promise offered by God in baptism does not benefit infants until they embrace the promise by faith. Infant baptism in the Reformed tradition would see the individual baptised into future faith and repentance, in the same way as circumcision was a sign of repentance. Many Christian communities of faith have developed a second rite called confirmation, or profession of faith. This is an opportunity for the person baptised as an infant to make their personal confession of faith, which is the goal of baptism.

Reaffirmation of Baptism

The Scriptures teach that all believers are to be baptised. Baptism is a visible sign that speaks of the beginning of our faith journey. In the case of infant baptism, this act looks forward to God's continuing saving grace in the life of the individual, and in the case of believers' baptism, this act looks back to see God's work that has already begun.

Since life is a journey, we need to offer people an opportunity to publicly reaffirm their baptismal vows. There are many pastoral occasions for the renewal of promises made in baptism. Some examples would be people returning to the church after a period of estrangement, those who are transferring their membership from one congregation to another, individuals who are sick or dying, or a congregation undertaking a corporate act of renewal. In these various instances it can be an opportunity for people to reaffirm their faith and commitment to Christ in a public manner.

Infant Dedication

The historical origins of infant dedication are difficult to determine. However, justification for this rite is found in several biblical texts. There is the presentation of Jesus at the temple when he was eight days old and blessed by Anna and Simeon (Luke 2:22–38). Many will reference Samuel's dedication to the Lord by his mother, Hannah; however, this was specifically the fulfillment of a vow made by Hannah committing her son to the Nazarite vow (1 Samuel 1:11). Finally, there is the reality of Jesus blessing children who were brought to him by their parents (Matthew 19:13–14).

As a spiritual practice, infant dedication is usually observed in churches that do not practice infant baptism. This act of dedication looks forward to the time when the child, having been raised in a godly environment, is able to make their own profession of faith. This profession of faith is then followed by the act of baptism, referred to as "believer's baptism."

In many respects infant dedication is very similar to infant baptism. Liturgist and theologian Richard Leonard states,

> The language and thrust of child dedication is similar to that found in the infant baptism services of many churches. Since the child who is being baptised is unable to confess faith in Christ, the parents do so in his or her behalf, and pledge themselves along with the congregation to provide a Christian environment to influence the maturing child. This environment will eventually lead to an adult commitment to Christ and his or her church through an act such as confirmation or covenanting. Exactly the same purpose is served in the rite of child dedication, except the commitment of the parents is to be ratified later in life not in confirmation or church membership but in believer's baptism.[41]

Discussion Questions about the Meaning and Practice of Baptism

The first sacrament that we will consider is baptism. The sacraments/ordinances are regarded as outward signs of God's inward work of grace.

Baptism

Read Matthew 28:16–20.

7–1. This is referred to as the Great Commission of Jesus. What are the four commands given by Jesus?

---

41. Richard Leonard, "A Theology of Child Dedication" in *Sacred Actions of Christian Worship*, vol. IV, ed. Robert Webber (Nashville: Star Song, 1994), 269.

How are they to make disciples? What resources do they have? What is the end goal?

Read Romans 6:1–14.

7–2. In this passage, we begin to understand the meaning of baptism. What does the symbolism suggest? How does this relate to the way we live as baptised followers of Jesus?

What does it mean that we are now dead to sin? What are the practical outcomes?

Read Acts 2:37–41.

7–3. This account is on the day of Pentecost, when people heard the word of God and repented of their sins, and about three thousand were baptised.

What does baptism signify in this instance? Why is it important as a sign of belonging to the community of faith?

What does baptism signify in your life?

8.
THE LORD'S SUPPER

Introduction

The Lord's Supper is the central act of our worship. It was the final meal shared by Jesus with his disciples prior to the crucifixion, and then it became the focus of the worship service in the early church.

Although Jesus did not specify how often we are to celebrate this meal, there seems to be apostolic precedent for the Lord's Supper being celebrated weekly (Acts 20:7). In this context we are told "they devoted themselves to the apostles' teaching, and to the fellowship, to the breaking of bread and to prayer" (Acts 2:42).

Background

The Lord's Supper is clearly linked with the Passover feast. Passover was a reminder to the people of Israel that God had delivered them from Egypt, the land of bondage and slavery, into the promised land of freedom. In a similar manner, the Lord's Supper is a reminder of the freedom we have from the bondage of sin and the promise of abundant and eternal life through the sacrifice when Christ gave his life for us.

Names of the Sacrament

The Lord's Supper

This is the most common name in Protestant churches. The major emphasis is on the fact that this is a supper instituted by Jesus, and he invites us to come as his guests.

The Breaking of Bread

This name suggests the action of Jesus breaking the bread as a symbol that his body would be broken. The Christian brethren use this term (Acts 2:42; 20:7).

The Eucharist

This term means thanksgiving/blessing and is taken from the text where Jesus took the bread and blessed it and then took the cup and gave thanks (Matthew 26:26–27).

Holy Communion

This term refers to the fact that as the people of God, when we celebrate the sacrament, we do so as a people set apart unto God (holy) and we celebrate this act together (communion) (1 Corinthians 11:27–34).

Biblical scholar N. T. Wright states,

> The fact that the church has developed different names for this event is an indication that we all know it is important and are anxious to interpret it correctly … Jesus used his final meal with his followers not only as a way of explaining what his forthcoming death would mean, but as a way of enabling them to share in that death, making it quite literally a part of their life through eating the bread and drinking the wine.[42]

The Meaning of the Lord's Supper

There are several meanings implied in the sacrament, but we will consider only a few. It will require further study to understand the depth and fullness of these different meanings.

The Lord's Supper represents the death of Christ. The words "my body broken for you, my blood shed for you" convey this message.

---

42. Wright, *The Day the Revolution Bagan*, 378.

As bread and wine nourish our bodies, so through our participation in this sacrament we are nourished spiritually by Christ. He is the one who gives us the spiritual strength we need for daily living.

In this celebration, we are aware of the symbolic intimacy we share with one another. This celebration reinforces the unity and communion within the body of Christ.

This sacrament assures every believer that all the promises and blessings of the gospel are theirs. In Christ we do possess eternal life.

Finally, as we eat the bread and drink the wine, we are professing that Christ is Saviour and Lord. And we will celebrate this sacrament until the day when we eat and drink with our Saviour when he comes again in power and glory (1 Corinthians 11:26).

Understanding the Real Presence of Jesus

Within the Reformed tradition, the tradition I am associated with, the celebration of the Lord's Supper is far more than simply remembering Jesus and his death for our sins. Rather, as Calvin taught, Christ is truly present with us. The celebration of the Passover meal is more than just remembering what happened in the past. For the participants, it is a reliving of what happened. In this manner, we are caught up in God's saving work. Theologian Fleming Rutledge states,

> If we say the Lord's Supper is a "memorial," we do not mean that we are simply thinking about Jesus' last supper … When we repeat Jesus' words, "do this in remembrance of me," in the communion service, we do not simply call Jesus to mind. Jesus is actively present with power in the communion of the people. We are not just thinking about Jesus' actions in the upper room; we acknowledge that he is present and acting with the community gathered at the table at the present time.[43]

Therefore, when we participate in the Lord's Supper, we remember the sacrifice of Christ on the cross and share in his redeeming work, because Christ is present. Calvin would stress that in the sacrament "the Holy Spirit imbues believers with the risen Christ's spiritual reality."[44]

---

43. Fleming Rutledge, *The Crucifixion: Understanding the Death of Jesus Christ* (Grand Rapids: Eerdmans, 2015), 218.
44. Thomas Finger, *The Sacred Actions of Christian Worship* (Nashville: Star Song, 1994), 221.

There are other traditions within the evangelical community that understand this sacrament as a symbolic remembrance of Christ's death on the cross.

Who May Participate in the Sacrament?

To participate in the sacrament, people should recognize they are sinners undeserving of God's love and grace, repent of their sins, and trust in Christ alone for forgiveness. Thus, there is a need to make an authentic profession of faith.

The repentance of sin must be followed by a desire to follow Christ and to become more and more like him in our daily life.

Before taking the sacrament, each person ought to examine their life to determine if there is unconfessed sin that needs to be dealt with. Since we celebrate together, we need to make certain that our relationship with one another is right (1 Corinthians 11:17–34).

Many churches struggle with the question of whether or not to permit children at the table. Paul, in writing to the church, declares that a person ought to examine their life before they come to the table to ensure that they are in right communion with God and with each other. Consequently, there are some churches that believe children are not capable of this process of self-examination. Others will argue that if baptism is the rite into the church, we then deny this means of grace (the Lord's Supper) to help a young person grow in their faith (1 Corinthians 11:28).

From a pastoral perspective, it important that children who are permitted to come to the table understand the meaning and significance of this sacrament at their level of maturity. And it is important that parents undertake their sacred responsibility in helping their child understand what it means practically to "discern the body."

Believers who are under church discipline may be excluded from participating in this sacrament.

Four Perspectives

Author and minister David Watson suggests that as we consider the Lord's Supper, it can be examined from four perspectives:[45]

We are called to look *back*, to remember what Christ has done freeing us from the bondage of sin.

We are to look *in* to examine our lives, to allow the Spirit of God to cleanse any area of our life that has residual sin.

We are to look *around* to recognize that we do not participate alone, but with one another in the community of faith. Therefore, we need to examine our relationships with one another.

We are to look *forward*, to realize that, as we eat the bread and drink the wine, we proclaim the Lord's death until he comes. All of this points to the celebration that will occur when Jesus returns at the end of time, and we will celebrate with him.

DISCUSSION QUESTIONS ABOUT THE SIGNIFICANCE OF THE LORD'S SUPPER

8–1. Jesus was preparing to celebrate Passover when he instituted this new celebration. What is the significance of Passover? (Read Exodus 12:25–29.) Do you see how Jesus incorporated this Old Testament feast in this new one? What are the similarities and the differences?

---

45. David Watson, *I Believe in the Church* (London: Hodder and Stoughton, 1982), 239.

As Jesus took bread and wine, what meaning did he give to these elements? What does it mean to recognize the "body of the Lord"?

Read 1 Corinthians 11:17–24.

8–2. In this passage, we see some instructions about participating in this feast. How were people distorting the feast? What does it mean to eat in an unworthy manner (verse27)? What does it mean to recognise the body of the Lord?

8–3. Paul states we are to examine ourselves before we participate in the feast (verse 28). What is involved in this process of self-examination?

8–4. Who should be participants in the Lord's Supper?

How does your participation strengthen your faith?

8–5. Some churches are wrestling with the question of permitting children to participate in the sacrament. What are your thoughts?

What biblical guidelines would help people come to a decision?

9.
LIVING THE CHRISTIAN LIFE

Introduction

A Christian is an individual who acknowledges Jesus Christ as Lord and Saviour and seeks to follow him in their daily life. The Bible speaks about being a disciple of Jesus, and this implies we are devoted to him and have responded to his call to "come and follow me" (Mark 1:17).

Maturing as a Christian

As a follower of Jesus, it is essential that one grows in their relationship with him. This is not an automatic process, but it is a journey we embark on every single day of our lives.

 Consider the following four specific areas:

Grow in Faith

Faith is learning to depend on God in every circumstance of life by taking him at his word and trusting his promises. Our faith needs to develop, and as we learn more about God and rely on him, our faith will increase, and we will trust him even more. The first disciples of Jesus learned this in the everyday experiences of life. At times Jesus spoke to them about how little faith they had (Matthew 8:26; Luke 17:5–6).

Grow in Love

Many would consider that love is the greatest thing in the world. In fact, the mark of a Christian is one who loves. Our love for God will be reflected in our love for others. Jesus declared, "Love one another. As I have loved you, so you must love one another. By this everyone will know that you are my disciples, if you love one another" (John 13:34–35). What we need to understand is that love is not so much a feeling as it is an action (John 13:1–17; 1 Corinthians 13:4–8).

Grow in Knowledge

Since there are many ideologies that call for your allegiance, it is important that Christians know what they believe and why they believe it. The journey of life is one of learning and making new discoveries. However, we are not simply talking about filling one's head with philosophical concepts; rather, growth in the knowledge of God implies living out the truth one has discovered. The apostle Paul writes, "We continually ask God to fill you with the knowledge of his will through all the wisdom and understanding that the Spirit gives, so that you may live a life worthy of the Lord and please him in every way: bearing fruit in every good work, growing in the knowledge of God" (Colossians 1:9–10).

Grow in Holiness

Holiness is a strange word for many. Our culture understands this word to convey a flavour of weirdness. The theological term for growing in holiness is sanctification. Simply stated, holiness implies being set apart. Therefore, as we grow in holiness, we see from a practical perspective that we seek to become more and more like Jesus in the relationship we have with him and with one another. In other words, we desire that the life of Jesus—the manner and way he lived—should be lived out in and through our lives. For such a transformation of our character, we need to yield to the work and influence of the Holy Spirit in this process (2 Corinthians 3:18; 1 Thessalonians 4:1).

Spiritual Practices

There are many different spiritual practices that have enabled followers of Jesus to grow and develop in their faith journey. This introduction to a few basic practices is intended to give you some insight that will provide you with practical ideas you can explore.

Spending Time in God's Word

Jesus said, "If you hold to my teaching, you are really my disciples. Then you will know the truth, and the truth will set you free" (John 8:31–32). It is important to read the Bible since it is God's word. It is through this means that God reveals himself to us and makes his ways known to his people.

Suggestions

Read the Bible systematically.

Read the Bible in different translations.

Choose a reading plan, and stick to it.

Most people become familiar with an inductive study plan, which asks three questions that use inductive reasoning. The questions are: *Observation*—what does the passage say? *Interpretation*—what does the passage mean? *Application*—how does the passage apply to my life? This is a helpful way to explore the Bible and to begin to appropriate the truth.

There is another method of reading the Bible which is to *meditate* on the passage. This is a way to appropriate the Word of God and apply it to life. Christian meditation is rooted and grounded in the Scriptures and involves a pondering and reflecting upon the word of God. God told Joshua, "Keep this Book of the Law always on your lips; meditate on it day and night, so that you may be careful to do everything written in it. Then you will be prosperous and successful" (Joshua 1:8).

Psychologist Siang-Yang Tan and theologian Douglas H. Gregg define meditation as

> the process of thinking through language that takes place in the heart or inner life. The truth meditated upon moves from the heart to the mouth (murmuring) to the mind (reflective thinking) and finally to the heart (outward action). The person meditating seeks to understand how to relate biblical truth to life.[46]

46. Siang-Yan Tang and Douglas H. Gregg, *Disciplines of the Holy Spirit* (Grand Rapids: Zondervan, 1997), 86.

Prayer

Through prayer, we seek to develop a greater intimacy with God. However, many find it difficult to pray. What do I say? Do I simply recite prayers that have been handed down for generations? Is my prayer simply a monologue whereby I tell God what is on my mind? Or is it a dialogue, which means listening to God as well as speaking?

Let me suggest some basic concepts that may help you to develop your life of prayer.

There are prayers of *adoration*. As you read the Psalms, you will discover attributes of God's character, which can lead to adoration. Or perhaps you will uncover the many promises God has made for his children. This too can lead to praise.

The following passages are examples that will help you express adoration and praise to God: Psalms 95, 98, 103, and 106.

There are prayers of *confession*. Confession is the recognition that we have sinned and done that which is wrong in the sight of God and that we need his forgiveness. John the apostle writes: "If we claim to be without sin, we deceive ourselves and the truth is not in us. If we confess our sins, he is faithful and just and will forgive us our sins and purify us from all unrighteousness" (1 John 1:8–9).

Many have found the prayer of *examination* to be helpful in maintaining an open relationship with God. The practice is quite simple. At the end of the day, take a few minutes to ponder the following questions and then formulate your answers into a prayer.

- *Awareness*: where was I aware of God's presence in my day?

- *Gratitude*: what am I grateful to God for in this day?

- *Confession*: is there anything I need to confess to God in this day?

There are prayers of *petition* or *intercession*. Most are familiar with these aspects of prayer. There are times when we pray for our family, friends, community, and country and present their needs before God. Perhaps the greatest intercessory prayers came from the lips of Jesus. He prayed for those who crucified him, asking the Father to forgive them. We are told that following his ascension to heaven, Jesus is our advocate before the Father, praying on our behalf (Luke 23:34; Romans 8:34). It is quite amazing to realize that Jesus is praying for you and me in this moment of time.

As you offer your prayers of intercession, remember that you are depending on God to act in a way that is consistent with his character and that he seeks only the good for your life. As we share every aspect of our life with God, we are deepening our relationship with him. Paul writes, "Do not be anxious about anything, but in every situation, by prayer and petition, with thanksgiving, present your requests to God. And the peace of God, which transcends all understanding, will guard your hearts and your minds in Christ Jesus" (Philippians 4:6–7).

There are prayers of *lament*. Many are not familiar with this type of prayer, but in essence, it is a response to the pain and struggles everyone faces in life. In this prayer, the individual is usually asking questions like *God, why is this happening to me?* and *How long will this situation last? God, where are you in the midst of my pain and struggle?* As you learn to share your struggles with God, prayer will reveal the authenticity of your relationship in that you can be completely candid and honest. Remember, many of the Psalms are prayers of lament (Psalm 44:11–13, 17–26; Psalm 77:1–9).

Listening to God

Prayer is not simply speaking to God but also learning to listen to God as he speaks to us. Some will find this a challenge simply because it is difficult in our busy world to learn to be still and listen to what God is speaking into our hearts. The Psalmist writes, "Be still, and know that I am God" (Psalm 46:10).[47]

Honour God with Your Giving

Everything we have in life is a gift from God, and he requires us to be good managers of our resources. There are several biblical guidelines that will help us understand God's perspective on giving.

---

47. For further information on listening prayer, see Joyce Huggett, *The Joy of Listening to God* (Downers Grove: InterVarsity Press, 1986).

Purpose of Giving

In a culture of affluence, many are not satisfied with what they have and continually want more, believing things they accumulate will bring happiness and satisfaction. As we learn to give generously, giving becomes an *antidote to greed* (1 Timothy 6:17–19).

Many believe that if they give, then there will be less for themselves. When we give to God, we are *strengthening our trust in him* (Proverbs 3:9–10).

As we give, we are making an *eternal investment* (1 Timothy 6:18–19).

Giving brings *happiness into our life*. In the early church, those who had much gave to those who had very little. It was stated that there was not a needy person in the Christian community (Acts 4:34).

Tithing

A tithe simply refers to 10 percent. In the Old Testament, the principle of tithing meant that the people gave a tithe of their earnings/income to support the work of God. Everything the people had was recognized by them as a gift from God. God asked that they return 10 percent to his work and that they would live as responsible stewards of the remaining 90 percent. This action revealed at least three things:

1. Tithing demonstrated that the person was putting God first and their needs/desires second (Deuteronomy 14:23).
2. Tithing expressed gratitude to God (Psalm 116:12).
3. To refuse to offer God a tithe was equivalent to robbing God (Malachi 3:8–10).

In the New Testament, under the new covenant, tithing is not required. However, when one considers the generosity of God in giving us his Son, our giving is simply a response of thanksgiving. New Testament teaching about giving involves several factors that are instructive as we think about what we are to give.

1. We are to give happily (2 Corinthians 9:7).
2. We are to give willingly (2 Corinthians 9:7; 8:12).
3. We are to give generously (2 Corinthians 8:3–4; 9:6).

The key to giving is that people "gave themselves first to the Lord" (2 Corinthians 8:5).

Participate in the Church Family

There is no such thing as a "lone wolf" Christian. God has designed us to live in community. In fact, the reality of our relationship with God is seen in our relationships with each other.

We need each other for a variety of reasons.

1. Together we can encourage each other. The journey of life is not easy, and we are called to companion each other (Ecclesiastes 4:9–10, 12; Hebrews 10:24).
2. God has given each of us spiritual gifts so that together we can mutually build each other up in our faith (1 Corinthians 12:12–26).
3. Our life together is a witness to the world that God's love and grace is transforming (John 17:21).

In the early church, the people gathered in small house churches. In this context, they were able to minister to one another. Today, many churches have small fellowship groups at the center of their community life. Cultural researchers David Kinnaman and Mark Matlock found that among many who became followers of Jesus, they "didn't learn to follow Jesus by having a lot of head knowledge about him (although having the right beliefs matter). Experiencing Jesus is found in a relational pathway with family, friends, and other people who love and experience Jesus."[48]

Read Acts 2:42–47. Take some time and reflect on the different ways your faith community mirrors the life of the early church.

> They devoted themselves to the apostles' teaching and to fellowship, to the breaking of bread and to prayer … They sold property and possessions to give to anyone who had need … They

48. David Kinnaman and Mark Matlock, *Faith for Exiles* (Grand Rapids: Baker Books, 2019), 54.

broke bread in their homes and ate together with glad and sincere hearts, praising God and enjoying the favour of all the people. And the Lord added to their number daily those who were being saved. (Acts. 2:42–47)

DISCUSSION QUESTIONS ABOUT THE PRACTICE OF LIVING THE CHRISTIAN LIFE

When a person becomes a follower of Jesus, a new life has begun. We are going in a new direction, so it is important to understand what is involved in living this new life.

In Acts 2:42–47, we read of four elements that were essential in the life of the followers of Jesus: teaching, prayer, the Lord's Supper, and fellowship—the basic practices of their spiritual journey.

Teaching

Being taught the word of God is essential to the development of one's relationship with God. Through the Bible, we discover the mind and heart of God. As we walk through life, the Bible is like a light shining on our path giving us guidance and direction from God. It tells the truth about who we are and reveals the changes God desires for us.

Read Matthew 13:1–9; 18–23.

9–1. What are the four types of soil? What are their unique characteristics, and what happens to the seed in each instance?

9–2. How do you think you can develop deep roots so that you will have a productive life? What will a productive life look like?

Prayer

When we read the Bible, God is speaking to us. When we pray, we are listening and speaking to God. It is about developing an intimate relationship with him as we speak face-to-face. In prayer, we express our love for God; we share with him our faults and failures, our disappointments and our needs. All of life is shared openly and honestly.

Read Matthew 6:5–15.

9–3. Some like to pray so that others can see their piety. What do you discover in verses 5 to 8 that is essential for your prayer life?

Verses 9–13: What are the concerns we present to God first? What are the personal concerns presented next? How would you express these in your own words?

Verses 14–15: What is the relationship between prayer and forgiveness?

The Lord's Supper

The first Christians celebrated the Lord's Supper weekly when they gathered for worship in their homes.

Read 1 Corinthians 11:23–32.

9–4. How would you explain the symbol of breaking the bread and the wine in the cup? What does it mean that we do this in remembrance? What are we proclaiming?

What are some of the cautions that one needs to consider before participating in this sacrament/ordinance?

Fellowship

As Christians we are not called to live in isolation. Rather, we are called to live life together.

Read Acts 4:32–35.

9–5. What are the qualities that mark this church? Why do you think they shared life in this way?

As you think about your community of faith, how does it measure up to this picture of the early church? What do you think needs to change so that there would be more sharing and concern for the needs of each other?

10.
LEADERSHIP

Introduction

Jesus said:

> "You are the salt of the earth." (Matthew 5:13)
> "You will be my witnesses." (Acts 1:8)
> "As the Father has sent me, I am sending you." (John 20:21)

As we read these words of instruction given to all the followers of Jesus, it is evident that Christianity, from the very beginning, was a led by ordinary people, referred to as the laity. However, when the laity became less and less active as the doers of ministry, the clergy took over their role on a professional basis. Sadly, full-time ministers became a distinct class instead of being fellow servants of Christ. This also led to a hierarchical system, which increased the distance between the laity and the clergy.

It is to be noted that the terms *laos* (laity) and *kleros* (clergy) denote the same and not different people. Paul, writing to the church in Corinth, states that all followers of Jesus are the people (*laos*) of God (2 Corinthians 6:16).

The apostle Peter declares we are "a chosen people [*laos*], a royal priesthood, a holy nation, God's special possession" (1 Peter 2:9).

Thus, ministry involves the work of all the people of God and not just a special group.

When the term *kleros* is used, it references those who share in the redemptive work of God, which includes all whom God has called to himself. Consequently, it does not refer to a separate group within the church separate from the laity (Colossians 1:11–12).

Leadership

Although everyone is to be involved in ministry, the apostle Paul acknowledges that Christ has given leadership gifts to the church to enable the community of faith to be equipped for their ministry and to be built up in their faith.

> Christ himself gave the apostles, the prophets, the evangelists, the pastors and teachers, to equip his people for works of service, so that the body of Christ may be built up until we all reach unity in the faith and in the knowledge of the Son of God and become mature, attaining to the whole measure of the fullness of Christ. (Ephesians 4:11–13)

As we explore the gifts of apostles and prophets, they had three essential responsibilities. First, they were to lay the foundation of the church (Ephesians 2:20). Second, they received and declared the revelation of God's Word (Acts 11:27–28). Third, they confirmed the true marks of an apostle through signs, wonders, and miracles (2 Corinthians 12:12).

Apostles

When we think of the term *apostle*, we usually assume it was a unique group of individuals. Actually, the term *apostle* has different meanings. Bible scholar John Stott argues that the term has three different meanings.[49] First, from *apostolos*, it means "to send," and in that sense all Christians are apostles, sent into the world as witnesses of Christ and to share in his mission.

Second, he contends apostles were sent out by the early church either as missionaries or on some other errand.

Third, there were the "apostles of Christ," a distinct group of individuals personally chosen by Jesus and witnesses of the fact that Christ had been raised from the dead. In referring to this third group, Stott states, "In this sense there are no apostles today."[50]

---

49. John Stott, *God's New Society* (Downers Grove: InterVarsity Press, 1979), 160.
50. Stott, *God's New Society*, 160.

Qualifications for Apostles

- They had to be with Jesus from his baptism to his ascension (Acts 1:12–26).
- They had received a personal call from Jesus (Mark 3:14).
- They were witnesses to the resurrection (Acts 1:22).
- They had power to work miracles (Acts. 2:43; 5:12).
- In addition to the original twelve disciples (Simon also known as Peter, James son of Zebedee, John, Andrew, Philip, Bartholomew, Matthew, Thomas, James son of Alphaeus, Thaddaeus, Simon the Zealot, Judas Iscariot), others were added to the apostolic order. For example:
  - Matthias, who replaced Judas, one of the original disciples, who hanged himself after he betrayed Jesus (Acts 1:26)
  - Barnabas (Acts 14:3–4)
  - James (Galatians 1:19)
  - Paul (Romans 1:1; 1 Corinthians 15:8–10)

The apostles not only had power and authority to proclaim the gospel, but they also had power and authority in the church:

To teach (Acts 2:42).
To heal (Acts 5:15–16).
To discipline (Acts 5:1–11).
To provide oversight (Acts 15:36).

Although most would agree this gift was unique to the early church and does not exist today in this restricted sense, Stott contends,

Once we have insisted, however that there are today no apostles of Christ with the authority comparable to that of the apostles Paul, Peter and John, it is certainly possible to argue that there are people with apostolic ministries of a different kind, including episcopal jurisdiction, pioneer missionary work, church planting, itinerant leadership, etc.[51]

---

51. John Scott, *The Message of Ephesians*, The Bible Speaks Today (Nottingham: Inter-Varsity Press, 1984).

Peter Wagner, a church growth expert and former professor at Fuller Theological Seminary, supports this argument, declaring that an apostle "can refer to an individual who is gifted by God to exercise leadership over a number of churches. This could refer to a moderator, bishop or superintendent."[52] This contemporary use of the term *apostle* is different from the original meaning.

Prophets

In the New Testament, there are many references to prophets and prophecy; in fact, Jesus is referred to as a prophet. He revealed the nature of God, exposed the sin of humankind, showed the way of salvation, and taught as one who had authority (Matthew 21:11; Luke 7:16; John 4:19).

There are other prophets noted in the New Testament:

> John the Baptist (Matthew 3:1–12)
> Zechariah (Luke 1:67)
> Agabus (Acts 11:27–28)
> Judas, Silas (Acts 15:32)
> The four daughters of Philip (Acts 21:9)

Prophecy has an element of prediction that enabled God's people to know what to do under certain circumstances. In other cases, it authenticated the prophet as God's representative. However, a prophet was also considered to be a person who spoke God's word into a contemporary context. Prophets were God's means of divine revelation. In the Old Testament, it was common that as prophets began to speak to the people, they would begin by declaring, "Thus says the LORD."

Stott contends that if we see a prophet as a means of direct revelation, we would need to add their words to Scripture. Then the church would need to listen to and obey what they say.[53] He also argues that Paul uses the term *prophet* in this sense and in this context. Therefore, this gift is no longer existent today. However, much like the argument for apostles, Stott explores the gift of prophet as a subsidiary gift. He states,

---

52. C. Peter Wagner, *Your Spiritual Gifts* (New York: Regal, 1982), 123.
53. Stott, *God's New Society*, 161.

Some see it as a gift of biblical exposition, an unusual degree of insight into the Word of God, so that by the ministry of the Holy Spirit modern "prophets" hear and receive the Word of God not as a fresh revelation but as a fresh understanding of the old. Others see it as a sensitive understanding of the contemporary world.[54]

Minister and author Leslie Flynn would affirm this. "Prophets instructed, warned, promised, rebuked. Though the future was often part of their prophetic utterances, their emphasis was historical, practical, and relevant to the contemporary conditions."[55]

Evangelists

Evangelists are individuals gifted in proclaiming and relating the gospel in such an effective manner that people under the influence of the Holy Spirit put their faith and trust in Jesus Christ as Lord and Saviour.

Thus, an evangelist is one who effectively proclaims the good news.

A typical example of an evangelist was Philip. A detailed account of his efforts is found in Acts 8:26–40. In this account, we discover that the evangelist was at the vanguard of Christianity. These individuals went where the message of Jesus had never been heard and proclaimed Jesus as Saviour of humankind. Most evangelists were itinerant ministers, and after they established a group of believers in one location, they would move to another. A pastor/teacher would remain with this group of young believers, helping them mature in their faith.

There were some evangelists who identified with a local congregation and remained there for a much longer period. Timothy was one such individual. Part of his work was to establish sound doctrine and godliness of life among the people he ministered to so that the church could be established and become strong in their life together.

Although the gift of evangelism is not given to everyone, everyone has a responsibility to be a witness for Christ (Acts 1:8).

54. Stott, *God's New Society*, 162.
55. Leslie Flynn, *19 Gifts of the Holy Spirit* (Colorado Springs: David C. Cook, 1982), 144.

Pastors/Teachers

Many Bible scholars understand pastor/teacher as one office of leadership in the church. The term *pastor* implies caring and protection over the church. The concept is based on a shepherd caring for the flock (Acts 20:28). There is also the role of teaching the word of God to the people. Thus, the pastor/teacher is one who cares for the people and who teaches them God's word.

There are two terms used to describe this role. The term *pastor* is not distinct from the terms *bishop* (*episkopos*) and *elder* (*presbuteros*). In fact, the terms are different ways of identifying the same people. When we speak of pastor, elder, or bishop, we are speaking of the same individual since there is no difference in their role (1 Timothy 3:2; Acts 20:28).

In today's church we see the role of elders expressed in the same manner. The first element of their leadership is to nurture the people of God through the teaching of God's word. The second element is to provide spiritual direction and oversight to the people under their care. Today some denominations refer to these individuals as teaching and ruling elders.

Deacons

While elders teach and provide spiritual care for the congregation, there is still much more ministry that needs to be done in the church. This was evident in the early stage of the church. In Acts 6, the apostles were aware of the physical needs of widows who were in their midst. However, they did not want to neglect their teaching ministry to look after these other needs. Therefore, they chose seven individuals full of the Holy Spirit and wisdom to serve in this area of need.

The term *deacon* means "one who serves." The full details of the responsibilities of a deacon are not outlined in the Scriptures. What seems to be emphasized is their character (1 Timothy 3:8–12) and the understanding that to serve in this capacity is a place of blessing and honour (1 Timothy 3:13).

Women in Ministry Leadership Roles

Much of the biblical story tends to focus on the role of male leadership, but in fact there are many examples of women in leadership, especially in the emerging early church. The following seven women serve as examples of some of the leadership roles that women had. Hopefully this overview provides a platform for further discussion about the role that men and women play in the life and work of the church. In addition, two books—*Paul and Gender: Reclaiming the Apostle's Vision for Men and Women in Christ* by Cynthia Westfall and *The Ministry of Women in the New Testament: Reclaiming the Biblical Vision for Church Leadership* by Dorothy Lee—will give you further insight into this topic.

The Four Daughters of Philip

These four young women served in a prophetic role. Luke, in writing the book of Acts, mentions that Paul went to Caesarea and stayed at the house of Philip the evangelist. Philip had four unmarried daughters who prophesied (Acts 21:8–9).

Junia

At the end of his letter to the church in Rome, Paul lists a number of individuals who helped him in ministry. Two that are mentioned as apostles are Andronicus and Junia. There does not seem to be any definitive evidence that they are husband and wife or brother and sister. However, they had been in ministry with Paul and he states that they were outstanding among the apostles, and in fact they were followers of Christ before he was converted (Romans 16:7).

Phoebe

Phoebe is listed as a deacon in the church. In this role she would be engaged in serving the community of faith (Romans 16:1).

Priscilla

Priscilla and her husband, Aquila, were leaders in the church. Paul describes them as his coworkers. In fact, their leadership was so significant that all the churches in the region were grateful for their ministry. Some would note that the order in which they are named, Priscilla and Aquila, suggests that Priscilla had the senior leadership role. The role they likely played was that of pastor/teacher (Romans 16:3).

DISCUSSION QUESTIONS ABOUT THE EMERGING LEADERSHIP OF THE CHURCH

Over the years, the church has organized itself in different ways. Jesus appointed the apostles, who were to bear witness about him and establish the early church. There were also others who served as prophets, evangelists, pastor/teachers, and deacons.

What is often forgotten is that God gave spiritual gifts to every believer so that together we minister to one another. Ministry is not to be left to a select group of individuals.

When we think of ministry, Jesus is our example of one who serves, and there are different ways we can serve God in everyday life.

Read Matthew 20:17–28.

> 10–1. As you consider the request in verses 20 and 21, how does the disciples' perspective on the kingdom differ from Jesus's? Why do you think the other ten disciples were so upset?

What is Jesus's perspective on the kingdom? How does it operate?

How does this passage help you understand the concept of serving?

Read John 13:1–17.

10–2. What is your understanding of foot washing in that culture? Why did none of the disciples pick up the basin and towel?

How does Jesus challenge their understanding of being a Christ follower (verses 12–17)? How do you see this being lived out in your life?

The Role of Elders

As we consider leadership in the church, the following biblical references will enable you to have this information at your fingertips.

The Bible teaches that the local congregation is under the direction of a plurality of elders. These individuals are responsible to the Lord as shepherds of the assembly and have final responsibility for the local church under God (Acts 14:23; 1 Timothy 5:17–18; Philippians 1:1).

1. Shepherd the Flock

Serving in all humility, elders are to guide, direct, guard, and protect the members of the body, seeking to meet their needs and assist in any way possible, warning against harmful influences and against false teachers (Acts 20:28; Matthew 23:1–3; Colossians 4:16; 1 Timothy 3:1–7).

2. Lead Through Example

Elders are to provide a scriptural role model and are to set a pattern before their congregants of a rightly ordered life with the single purpose of glorifying God (1 Timothy 5:17; 1 Peter 5:1–2).

3. Teach

Elders are to see that the congregation is taught through insightful and accurate biblical instruction and admonition (1 Timothy 3:2; Titus 1:9).

4. Refute Those Who Contradict Truth

Elders are to confront those who teach false doctrine or who continue in behaviour that is contradictory to biblical truth. Further, they must deal with those who would cause dissension within the community of faith (Acts 20:29–31; Titus 1:9).

5. Manage the Church of God

Elders are to provide oversight for the life of the congregation with the assistance of other godly leaders (1 Timothy 3:1–7; 5:7).

6. Pray for the Sick

Elders are to pray for the spiritual and physical well-being of the members of the congregation (James 5:14–16).

The Qualifications of Elders

Each elder ought to have the necessary spiritual qualifications as well as a sense of God's calling to ministry and possess the confidence of the congregation to provide leadership.

Read the following texts to discover the various qualifications. Keep in mind that all of us are on a journey and that no one has attained perfection in these areas.

> 1 Timothy 3:1–12
> Titus 1:6–9

In summary, the qualifications are as follows:

Blameless
Respectable
Temperate
Self-controlled
Hospitable
Able to teach
Free from the love of money
Not a recent convert
Holy
Disciplined
Holding to the word of God

10–3. As you consider the role of an elder in a local congregation, how does the information noted above assist you in selecting candidates to serve in this capacity?

10–4. What are some of your concerns about those who serve in this role?

10–5. Do you think some would refrain from serving because they could not live up to the expectations of the congregation? How would you address that issue?

10.6. What process do you follow in selecting individuals to this leadership role? To what extent does your congregation engage in prayer and fasting as they seek wisdom in making their choice?

CASTLE QUAY BOOKS

WWW.CASTLEQUAYBOOKS.COM

Marriage
preparation
workbook

DAVID SHERBINO
Foreword by Marion Goertz: Managing Director at Tyndale Family Life Centre

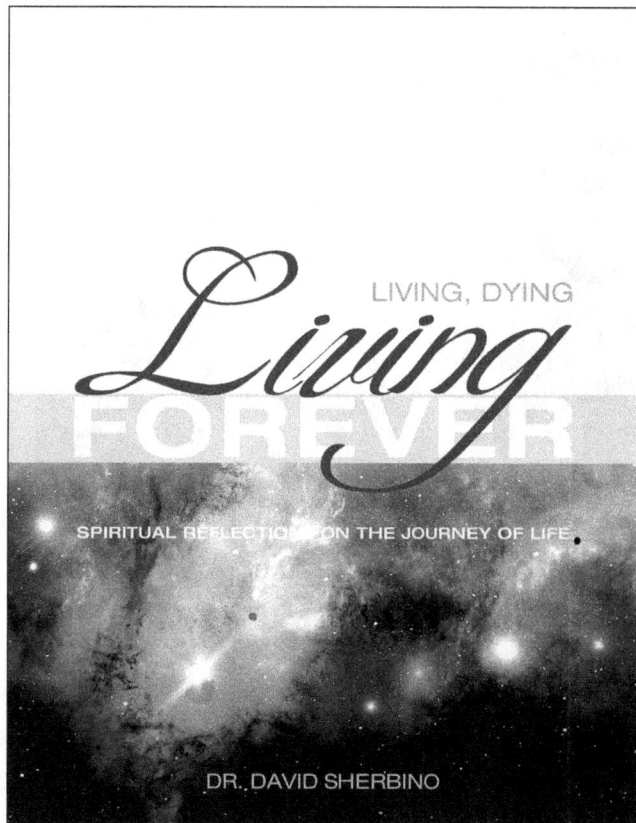

LIVING, DYING
Living
FOREVER

SPIRITUAL REFLECTIONS ON THE JOURNEY OF LIFE

DR. DAVID SHERBINO

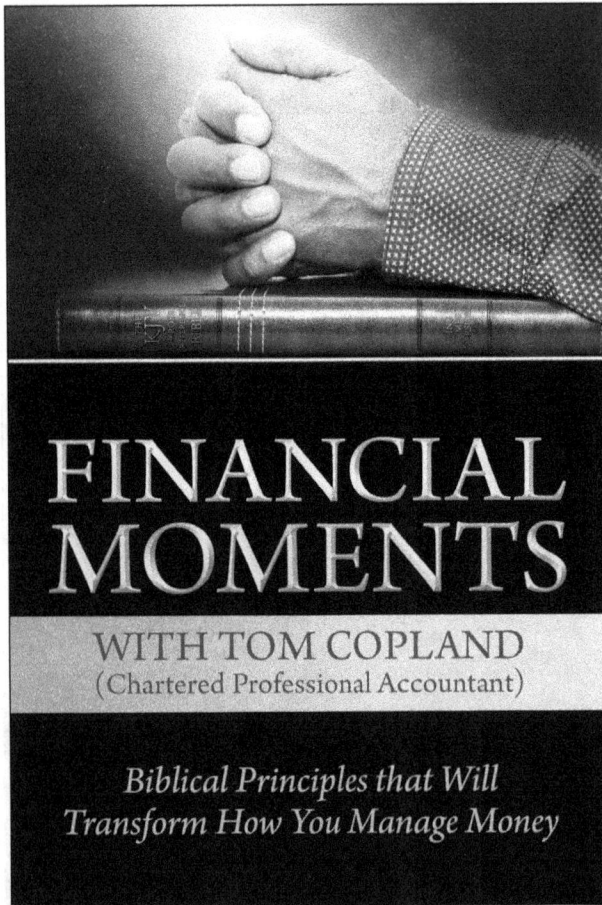

FINANCIAL
MOMENTS

WITH TOM COPLAND
(Chartered Professional Accountant)

Biblical Principles that Will
Transform How You Manage Money

CASTLE QUAY BOOKS
WWW.CASTLEQUAYBOOKS.COM

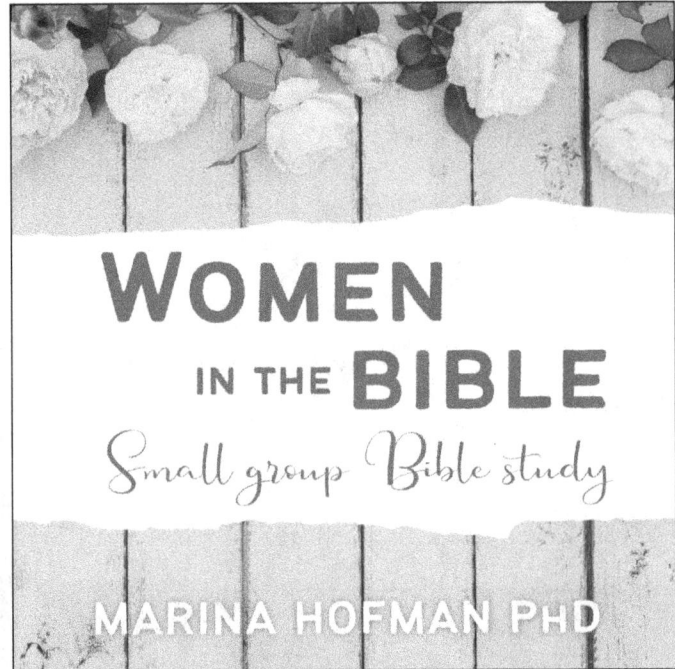

WOMEN
IN THE BIBLE
Small group Bible study

MARINA HOFMAN PHD

www.ingramcontent.com/pod-product-compliance
Lightning Source LLC
Chambersburg PA
CBHW062104090426

42741CB00015B/3321